The Unfortunate Luck of Sean O'Reilly

The Tale of the Whimsical Gold

SAMEER MEHRA

Genre: Comedy

ISBN: 978-93-6128-900-2
First Edition Published: March-2024
Cover Designed by: Sanjida Smrity

Index

Acknowledgments

I extend my heartfelt gratitude to my friends and family who have been a constant source of encouragement throughout this creative journey. Your belief in my storytelling abilities has been invaluable.

To my dear friends, your enthusiasm, feedback, and late-night brainstorming sessions enriched the story. Thank you for being my sounding boards and cheerleaders.

To my family, your patience and support during long hours of writing and editing have been invaluable. I am grateful for your love.

To the readers, I dedicate this book to you. Your curiosity and imagination inspire me.

Prologue

In the heart of Murphy's Forest stood a small but mighty figure: a leprechaun. Clad in vibrant green and with a face etched with tales of a thousand adventures, he was an extraordinary sight. The leprechaun, burdened by the endless responsibility of guarding a pot of gold, felt weary. He was longing for change, for someone to relieve him of his everlasting duty. With eyes lifted towards the sky, he whispered his wishes to the clouds, hoping for rain and a radiant rainbow to usher in a potential successor.

As he stood amidst the towering trees and rustling leaves, the leprechaun felt the weight of the gold and the many years he had spent safeguarding it. "I hope it rains today, a grand, magnificent rain," he muttered softly, his voice intertwining with the gentle whispers of the forest. "And then, may a brilliant rainbow stretch across the sky, its radiant arms reaching the ends of the earth."

He closed his eyes and envisioned the scene: the vibrant arch of colors lighting up the sky, heralding hope and guiding someone to this place of magic and mystery. "It's time for someone to find this pot of gold," he sighed. "I've carried its weight and tales for a lifetime. I yearn for rest, a pause from this endless adventure."

As if in response to his heartfelt plea, the sky began to transform. Dark clouds, heavy with promise, gathered, casting shadows that gently embraced the forest. The wind carried the melodies of change, swirling through each leaf and branch, touching every corner of Murphy's Forest with its refreshing breath. Soon, the awaited rain began to fall, each drop a symphony of relief and hope.

The drops of rain kissed the earth, dancing down leaves and petals, weaving paths of revitalization through the tired landscape. The leprechaun felt the rain touch his face, each drop a messenger of potential freedom from his age-old task. His heart lightened, and his feet began to move, inspired by the rhythm of the raindrops. In the midst of the forest's refreshed beauty, the leprechaun danced, his movements a blend of grace and ancient enchantment.

The dance was a mix of joy and anticipation. The leprechaun's feet tapped the soft, wet earth in harmonious beats, keeping rhythm with the rain's soothing melody. He twirled and swayed, allowing the rhythm of nature to flow through him, his mind filled with visions of rainbows and new beginnings.

As the rain nurtured the forest, breathing life into every tree and flower, the leprechaun continued to dance, hope igniting his spirit. He dreamed of the moment someone would step into the forest, guided by the rainbow's promise. He envisioned the treasure being found, the pot of gold passing on to new hands, allowing his own to finally rest.

The leprechaun's dance was a prayer, a powerful call to the forces of nature and magic. He sought the unfolding of a new chapter, one where the gold could find a new guardian, and he could find solace from his enduring responsibility. Encircled by the beauty of the refreshed Murphy's Forest and the rhythmic embrace of the rain, the leprechaun danced, awaiting the arrival of change and the freedom it would bring.

The Unfortunate Luck of Sean O'Reilly

Chapter 1

The Lopsided Chronicles of Limeridge

Limeridge was a quaint and tranquil town, characterized by its simple architecture and narrow, cobblestone streets. The houses were modest, mostly one or two stories high, painted in soft, earthy tones that blended seamlessly with the natural surroundings. The town center boasted a small marketplace, a few local shops, and a cozy diner where residents would gather to chat over coffee and homemade pastries. Gardens filled with flowers and herbs adorned the front yards, while the backyards often had small vegetable patches.

The town was surrounded by open fields and patches of woodland, offering a picturesque view from almost every angle. A small river meandered through the outskirts, its gentle flow a perfect symbol of the town's unhurried pace of life.

Beyond the town lay the Slothmore hills, an expanse of rolling hills that seemed to stretch lazily under the wide sky. These hills were covered in a thick blanket of green, with clusters of trees dotting the landscape. In the spring, wildflowers would bloom across the hills, creating a tapestry of colors that was a feast for the eyes. The hills were named 'Slothmore' because of their gentle slopes and the sense of peaceful slowness they imparted.

The paths winding through Slothmore were well-trodden by the townsfolk, often used for relaxed walks or picnics. The air there was fresh and crisp, filled with the scents of grass and earth. On clear nights, the hills provided the perfect backdrop for stargazing, with the vast, star-filled sky seeming almost within reach.

Together, Limeridge and the Slothmore hills existed in harmonious simplicity, a haven for those who cherished a life of tranquility and routine. The beauty of this place was in its unspoiled nature, the slow rhythm of life, and the comfort of the familiar. It was a world away from the rush and noise of the cities, a small pocket of peace where time seemed to move at its own leisurely pace.

Sean O'Reilly was a very different and fun person in the quiet town of Limeridge. Unlike the other people in town, who liked things calm and simple, Sean was always full of surprises and made everyone laugh. He didn't look like everyone else in town either.

Sean often wore mismatched clothes that looked like he had put them on in a hurry. His hair was always a bit messy, as if he had just gotten out of bed. He had a funny way of always looking surprised or confused, which made people smile. His nose was a bit crooked, like it had its own funny personality. And his glasses were always slipping down his nose, making him look even more amusing.

People in Limeridge could always tell when Sean was around because something funny was bound to happen. He might accidentally trip over a stone while walking, or would spill his coffee in a goofy way. But he always laughed at himself, and his laughter was so infectious that others couldn't help but laugh too.

Sean liked to tell jokes and funny stories. He had a knack for making even the most boring day interesting. When he walked into the local diner, the place would light up with his energy. He greeted everyone with a big smile and often had a funny story to share about his latest mishap.

In a town where every day was predictable, Sean was like a breath of fresh air. His cheerful attitude and silly mistakes brought a little bit of excitement to Limeridge. He was the kind of person who reminded everyone that it's okay to be different and that life doesn't always have to be serious. With Sean around, there was always a reason to smile in Limeridge.

Chaos Whiskerpaws, Sean's cat, was just as unique and lively as Sean himself. This cat wasn't like your regular house cat. Chaos had a thick, fluffy coat of fur that was a mix of black, white, and gray, looking almost like a little storm cloud. His eyes were bright green, always sparkling with mischief.

Chaos was known for his playful and curious nature. He would often chase after leaves or jump at shadows, adding to the amusement of Sean's adventures. This cat could turn anything into a toy – from a simple string to a rolling apple from the market. His antics were always a source of laughter and surprise.

Despite his playful behavior, Chaos was very smart and loyal to Sean. He seemed to understand when Sean needed company and would curl up beside him, purring loudly. But when Sean was up to his usual fun, Chaos was right there with him, adding to the excitement.

Chaos had a habit of climbing on things he shouldn't, like the top of fences, the roofs of houses, or even sitting daringly on the edge of the town's fountain. He could balance himself in the most unexpected places, surprising everyone who saw him.

In Limeridge, where every day was predictable, Chaos was another delightful exception. People would often find him in the most unexpected places, like snoozing in a basket at the marketplace or playfully pouncing on fallen leaves in the park.

Together, Sean and Chaos were a remarkable pair. Their presence in Limeridge was like a little spark of joy and unpredictability. They brought fun and laughter wherever they went, making the ordinary days in Limeridge a bit more extraordinary.

Chapter 2

The Day of the Great Pudding Pandemonium

A particularly memorable day in the history of Limeridge was the day of the annual Pudding Contest, a day that would forever be known as 'The Day of the Great Pudding Pandemonium.' Sean decided he wanted to join the contest. He found an old family recipe for pudding, but it was a bit strange and made him scratch his head.

Before starting, he had a hilarious chat with his cat, Chaos Whiskerpaws. It went something like this:

"Alright, Whiskers," Sean said, holding up the recipe like a treasure map. "Today's the day we make history with this pudding!"

Chaos looked at him with those big green eyes, probably thinking, 'What are you up to now?'

Sean continued, "This recipe is a bit... well, weird. But I'm sure we can make it work. It'll be the best pudding Limeridge has ever seen!"

Chaos meowed as if to say, 'Are you sure about this?'

"You just wait and see, Whiskers. We'll mix and stir and maybe cause a little mess, but it's going to be great. Who knows, we might even win!"

Chaos purred, probably thinking about all the fun mess that was about to happen.

Sean laughed and said, "Okay, team huddle. Our mission: create an epic pudding and have fun doing it. Are you with me?"

Chaos bumped his head against Sean's leg, which was his way of saying, 'Let's do this!'

So, Sean rolled up his sleeves and got ready for the pudding-making adventure. He was determined to make the best pudding for the contest, even if it meant turning the kitchen upside down. And with Chaos by his side, it was sure to be a day filled with laughter and a whole lot of chaos.

Making pudding in Sean's kitchen was no ordinary task, especially on the day of the annual Pudding Contest in Limeridge. It wasn't just about mixing ingredients. Oh no, it was a full-blown performance, a spectacle of spontaneous surprises and unintended hilarity. The audience, or should I say, the kitchen, witnessed a spectacular performance that would be remembered for its unconventional approach and the unforgettable mess it created.

First, imagine the ingredients acting like they had minds of their own. Flour would poof into the air, creating a mini snowstorm right in the middle of the kitchen. Eggs, those slippery little things, seemed to play a game of 'how fast can we roll off the counter.' Sometimes they'd land with a splat on the floor, and other times they'd somehow end up in the most unexpected places, like on top of the fridge!

Milk was another story. It liked to pretend it was part of a splashy water show, jumping out of the bowl whenever Sean wasn't looking. Sugar was like a little artist, leaving sweet, powdery trails everywhere.

Sean, who was in charge of this wild show, was like a conductor in an orchestra, only his orchestra was made up of kitchen utensils and ingredients. He'd try to mix things in a bowl, but the bowl seemed to have its own ideas, spinning like a merry-go-round, especially if Sean got too enthusiastic with his stirring.

Then there was Chaos, the cat. He didn't believe in things like 'recipes' or 'the right way to do things.' To him, the kitchen was a playground. He'd jump onto the counter with a flair, pawing at the rolling eggs or trying to catch the flying flour. Sometimes, he'd sit and watch, his tail swishing back and forth, as if he was thinking, "What will Sean do next?"

Sean would often talk to Chaos as if he understood every word. "Ah, Whiskers, do you think we need more sugar? Maybe it will make the pudding extra special!" Chaos would meow, and Sean would take it as agreement, adding another heap of sugar.

Mixing the ingredients was like a dance – a very funny, clumsy dance. Sean would try to follow the steps of the recipe, but more often than not, he'd end up adding his own twist. "A pinch of this, a splash of that," he'd say, often resulting in unexpected flavors and textures.

The kitchen was a scene of joyful chaos. Pots and pans clanged like cymbals in an orchestra. The mixer, which Sean sometimes struggled to control, would whirr and buzz, sometimes flinging batter in artistic patterns across the walls.

As for the pudding itself, it was anyone's guess how it would turn out. Each step of the process was an adventure. Would the milk and eggs blend smoothly, or would they decide to form a mini tsunami? Would the flour behave, or would it decide to decorate the kitchen and Sean in a fine, white dusting?

In the midst of all this, Sean would laugh heartily, his laughter echoing through the kitchen, adding to the cheerful cacophony. He knew that winning the contest wasn't really the point. It was about having fun, creating something unique, and enjoying the hilarious journey along the way.

By the time the pudding was in the oven, the kitchen looked like it had been through a fun but very messy storm. Flour footprints, eggshell art, and a splattering of various ingredients decorated the room. But in that mess, there was a sense of accomplishment and a lot of happy memories.

In the end, the unmatched duo: Sean and Chaos, managed to create something wild and wonderful in the kitchen. Calling it a pudding, though, that might be a stretch. It was a concoction, a mysterious brew that looked like it had as many secrets as a haunted mansion. The "dessert," if we dare call it that, seemed to be a delightful disaster that had a mind of its own, ready to surprise or perhaps even shock anyone daring enough to try it.

Word spread quickly across the town, and soon, a crowd gathered, curious to witness Sean's latest extraordinary endeavor. The pudding that Sean made was a sight to see, and it sure did catch everyone's attention in

Limeridge. When it was time to show it off, people gathered around, curious to see what Sean had cooked up this time.

Well, the pudding was... interesting. It wasn't like any pudding most people had seen before. It wobbled and jiggled like a bouncy castle, as if it had a life of its own. The colors were a mix of everything you can imagine - there were spots of pink, swirls of green, and even some mysterious blue streaks. It looked like a rainbow had melted into a bowl!

The top of the pudding had a sprinkle of everything - from nuts that looked like they were trying to escape to bits of fruit that seemed to be swimming in the jiggly sea. And there were these little silver sparkles on top, making it look like a disco ball at a party.

The shape of the pudding was funny too. It wasn't smooth and round like normal puddings. Instead, it had lumps and bumps, making it look like a mini pudding mountain range. It was as if the ingredients decided to have a dance party and then froze in place when they were done.

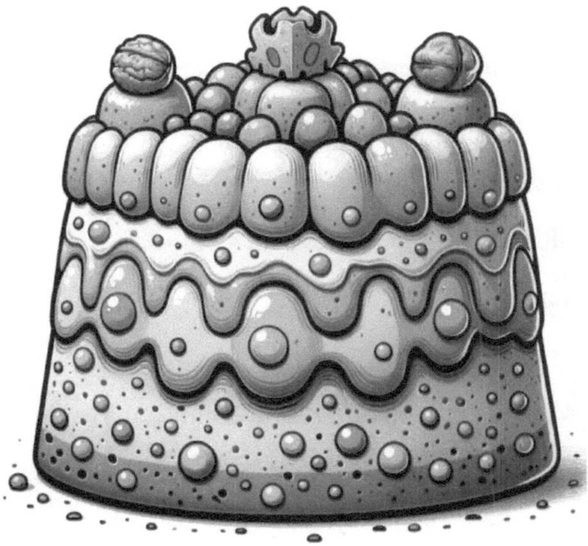

When Sean brought it out, the pudding wobbled so much that everyone took a step back, half-expecting it to leap out of the bowl. Some people in the crowd couldn't help but laugh, and others just stared, their eyes wide with surprise and curiosity.

Sean, proud as ever, presented the pudding with a big grin. "Behold, the masterpiece!" he declared. And Chaos, his cat, sat beside him, looking at the pudding as if he was thinking, 'Did we really make that?'

The sight of the pudding made everyone in Limeridge forget about being proper and serious. Instead, they laughed and joked, making up funny names for what the pudding could be called. It was a moment filled with joy and silliness, all thanks to Sean's one-of-a-kind pudding creation.

The moment had arrived. The room held its breath as spoons were armed and aimed at the mysterious mound known as "the pudding." It was the kind of hushed silence that falls over an audience just before the curtains swoosh open to reveal the wonders of a stage show. But this wasn't any old stage show; oh no, this was the Great Pudding Performance!

The clock struck taste-time! Everyone was on the edge of their seats, eyes wide open, spoons at the ready. What happened next was not just a tasting; it was a culinary explosion, a fiesta of flavors firing in all directions. The pudding, possibly feeling the pressure of the spotlight, decided to give a performance of its own. BOOM! It exploded!

It wasn't your average, everyday explosion. It was a fantastical firework of custard and fruit, a volcanic eruption of sweet, gooey madness. A cascade of colorful dessert debris rained down, showering the room in a wild whirlwind of whacky ingredients. People ducked, dodged, and dove as the room transformed into a battleground of flying fruits and zooming zest.

Faces became canvases as the ingredients created masterpieces of slapstick art. Glasses were not spared as they became pools of custard, and hair turned into messy marvels of fruity fashion. A gentleman found himself wearing a custard hat, and a lady sported a new, rather avant-garde, fruity scarf.

One adventurous cherry zoomed across the room, aiming straight for Mr. Johnson's open mouth as he gasped in surprise. Score! Direct hit! Meanwhile, a mischievous strawberry played peek-a-boo in Mrs. Smith's hair, turning her into an accidental fruit salad fashionista.

In the midst of this sweet chaos, the pudding sat—or what was left of it—in the center of the table, looking rather pleased with its grand spectacle. It had turned the tasting into a full-blown comedy show, leaving the room and its inhabitants in a delightful disarray of dessert decor.

The air buzzed with echoes of laughter and gasps, creating a symphony of reactions to the pudding's unexpected performance. It was a moment out of a slapstick comedy, a scene that would be remembered for its unexpected surprises and joyful jest. The pudding, the star of the show, took a bow, leaving the audience covered in applause—or rather, a colorful array of dessert remnants!

This incident became yet another legendary tale in the life of Sean O'Reilly, Limeridge's unintentional comedian. Sean, with Chaos by his side, managed to turn a mundane event into an unforgettable experience, filling the town's ordinary existence with stories of excitement, humor, and delightful chaos. Their presence brought a much-needed breath of fresh air to Limeridge, turning everyday experiences into extraordinary tales filled with laughter and unexpected surprises. In their own unique way, Sean and Chaos introduced a sense of joy and spontaneity to the town's otherwise predictable lifestyle, leaving behind stories that would be cherished and retold for generations to come.

Chapter 3

Sean's Rainbow Rendezvous

Last night, it rained really hard in Limeridge, like a big thunderstorm was passing through. But the next morning, everything was calm and peaceful. Sean O'Reilly, who always finds himself in funny situations, woke up and made his morning coffee. When he stepped outside, he saw something amazing in the sky.

There was a rainbow, and it was like no other rainbow Sean had ever seen. It was so bright and colorful that it looked like it came out of a fairy tale. The colors were so strong and clear – bright reds, oranges, yellows, greens, blues, indigos, and violets. It was as if a unicorn with a paintbrush had dashed across the sky, leaving this trail of colors behind.

The rainbow was huge, stretching from one end of the sky to the other. It looked like a giant colorful bridge connecting the earth to the sky. The colors seemed to dance and shimmer, almost like they were alive. The red looked like a cherry, the orange like a blazing sunset, the yellow like a sunflower, the green like fresh grass, the blue like the deepest ocean, the indigo like a twilight sky, and the violet like a field of lavender.

Sean just stood there for a while, looking up at this incredible rainbow. His eyes moved from one color to the next, trying to take in all the beauty. He was so used to funny mishaps and chaos, but this moment was just peaceful and beautiful. It was like the rainbow was putting on a show just for him.

For a guy who usually found himself in the middle of delightful disasters, this was a pleasant change. It was a reminder that sometimes, right after a big storm, you get something as wonderful as a bright, beautiful rainbow. It was a perfect start to Sean's day, filling him with awe and a bit of wonder.

Sean O'Reilly stepped into a world full of bright and chaotic rainbows, his eyes full of dreams and curiosity. With him was his trouble-making cat, Chaos Whiskerpaws, always ready for mischief and adventures.

Sean, wearing his big goofy glasses that always seemed a bit too big for his face, turned to look at his cat, Chaos.

The glasses slid down his nose as he spoke, making him look even goofier.

"Chaos," he said, his voice full of amazement as he pointed at the rainbow, "do you see that? It's like a giant, colorful carpet in the sky!"

Chaos looked up, his green eyes following where Sean was pointing. He meowed, as if he was trying to say, 'Wow, that's something!'

Sean laughed and pushed his glasses back up his nose. "It's not just any carpet, though. It's like the kind of carpet a king would have, only even more colorful. And look at the colors! They're so bright and cheerful, like they're inviting us on an adventure."

He imagined the rainbow as a path leading to a treasure, and his eyes sparkled with excitement. "I bet at the end of that rainbow, there's a pot of gold. And not just any gold, but gold coins that jiggle and dance!"

Chaos tilted his head, looking a bit puzzled, as if he was trying to figure out how gold coins could jiggle and dance.

"You know, like those coins in video games, bouncing up and down," Sean explained with a grin. "Imagine us finding a pot full of those! We'd be rich! Rich enough to buy all the cat treats in the world for you, Whiskers!"

Chaos purred and rubbed against Sean's leg, probably liking the sound of unlimited cat treats.

Sean continued, his imagination running wild. "We could be like pirates, searching for treasure. You could be Captain Chaos, the most feared and adorable pirate cat on the seven seas!"

Chaos stared back, whiskers wiggling as if trying to do the hula dance, giving a meow that echoed like a cryptic clue in a game show. Sean nodded, taking the meow as a sign, a profound purr-proval of his wild imagination. "Just think of it, Chaos," Sean's mind whooshing into the wonderland, "a pot full of gold waiting for us, twinkling like a disco ball!"

Sean's imagination, always ready to put on a show, did a somersault. "Imagine swapping our dull days for a dazzling dreamland. Plush pillows puffier than marshmallows, and shiny chandeliers flickering like a smile in a soap opera!"

Chaos purred, an engine revving sound that seemed to fuel Sean's already racing imagination. "How about a magical castle for you, Chaos? A fabulous feline fortress where every corner is a cuddle party. Treats tumbling down like confetti, and yarn balls unwinding tales of tantalizing tuna."

The drama didn't end there. Sean's mind was like a theater, and his thoughts, the overacting actors. Visions of gold coins danced in his head, a conga line of endless extravagance and elegance.

Motivated by this cinematic spectacle of imagination and the mysterious meows from his buddy Chaos, Sean made up his mind. "Let's dive into this delightful disaster," he declared, "Chasing the rainbow, like cats chasing laser dots, and who knows, we might just stumble upon a jackpot of joy!"

Sean and “Captain” Chaos, on the way to their adventure walked through the village, Sean told everyone they met about their treasure hunt. "We're off to find the gold at the end of the rainbow!" he'd announce with a big smile. People in the village just laughed and shook their heads. They were used to Sean's funny ideas.

"Good luck, Sean! Don't get lost!" someone called out. Another person joked, "Bring back some of that gold for us too!"

Sean just laughed and waved. "Will do! We'll share the treasure with everyone!"

Chaos meowed, strutting alongside Sean like a little furry captain. He seemed to enjoy all the attention they were getting.

As they followed the rainbow, it looked like it was leading them to Murphy's Forest. Sean had always been curious about this forest. It was a bit mysterious and nobody in the village went there much. But Sean thought it was the perfect place for a hidden treasure.

When they reached the entrance of the forest, Sean couldn't help but jump around in excitement. He looked like a kangaroo that had eaten too much sugar. "This is it, Chaos! The forest of mystery and adventure! Who knows what we'll find in here?"

Chaos looked at the forest and then at Sean, his tail twitching. He seemed to say, 'Well, as long as you're going in, I'm following you!'

"So, buddy, are we going on a wild treasure hunt or what?" Sean chuckled, looking down at Chaos, who looked ready to dive into some mischief. Their hearts puffed up like giant balloons, filled with goofy dreams and ridiculous hopes.

They marched on like two clowns in a parade, imagining a jackpot of leprechaun gold or maybe a hurricane of hilarious hiccups waiting for them. But hey, who's keeping track? They were out for a blast, strapped into a wild rollercoaster of craziness, zooming into zany zigzags without any brakes!

"Ready to dive into the wacky unknown, Chaos?" Sean said, feeling like a kid opening a surprise present. Off they went on their ridiculous rainbow road trip, stepping into a funhouse of surprises, where every corner might be hiding a bucket of laughs or a confetti explosion of adventure!

Chapter 4

A Frolic through Murphy's Forest

In the mystical Murphy's Forest, where nature's tales are woven into the fabric of reality, Sean O'Reilly, accompanied by his insightful cat, Chaos, embarked on an extraordinary adventure. Guided by the soft hues of a revealing rainbow, they traversed the wonder-filled pathways, where each step echoed with the whispers of ancient tales and the rhythmic songs of the surreal forest life.

Sean, driven by a heart filled with curiosity and enthusiasm, explored the forest's enchanting terrains with playful vitality, akin to a joyful squirrel. His steps resonated with excitement, moving gracefully over the forest's intricate tapestry of ferns and fungi. "Look, Chaos," Sean exclaimed, filled with a sense of delight and wonder, "we are on a marvelous journey to uncover the forest's well-kept secrets!"

Chaos, the cat, moved with an effortless curiosity, embodying a sense of mysterious wisdom. With smooth and elegant movements, the cat explored the vibrant wilderness, embracing the symphony of life and mystery that played in the heart of the forest.

As Sean and Chaos walked deeper into Murphy's Forest, it was like they were in a magical nature show. Everything around them seemed to be alive and part of their adventure.

The branches of the trees swayed back and forth as if they were dancing to a song only they could hear. The wind whistled through the leaves, making a soft, gentle music. It was as if the trees were cheering Sean and Chaos on their treasure hunt.

The sunlight peeked through the leaves, creating patterns on the ground that looked like golden puzzle pieces. Sean joked, "Look, Chaos, the sun is playing hide and seek with us!"

Chaos would chase the spots of sunlight, trying to catch them with his paws. It was funny to watch him pounce and then look confused when there was nothing to catch.

As they walked, Sean and Chaos found all sorts of little treasures. They saw a bird’s nest with baby birds waiting for their mother. Sean said, "See, Chaos, they're waiting for their treasure too – breakfast!"

They found a stream with water so clear, you could see the pebbles at the bottom. Sean pretended the pebbles were precious gems. "We've found the diamond creek!" he exclaimed.

Chaos, curious as ever, tried to catch the water with his paws, but it just splashed around, making him look surprised each time.

Butterflies fluttered around them, their colorful wings like little flying flowers. Sean laughed and said, "Maybe these are the forest fairies, guiding us to the treasure."

Even the squirrels joined in their adventure. They'd run up and down the trees, chattering as if they were telling Sean and Chaos to hurry up or they'd miss the gold.

The whole forest felt like it was part of their journey. Every leaf, every bird, every ray of sunlight added to the fun and excitement. It was like nature was playing along, turning their treasure hunt into a wonderful exploration.

As Sean and Chaos ventured further into the forest, a delightful array of mysterious and wonderful experiences unveiled themselves. The environment seemed alive with playful shadows, whimsical winds, and the cheerful songs of birds, creating a vivid canvas of experiences, filled with laughter and the essence of life's beautiful unpredictabilities.

Walking through Murphy's Forest, Sean's imagination was running wild. He started talking to Chaos about all the fun and silly things he would do if they really found a pot of gold at the end of the rainbow.

"Okay, Whiskers," Sean said, stepping over a log with a big grin on his face, "imagine we find this pot of gold. What should we do with it?"

Chaos meowed and twitched his tail, as if he was really listening.

"First thing," Sean continued, "we'll buy a lifetime supply of cat treats for you. You'll have a mountain of treats, and you can spend all day every day deciding which one to eat!"

Chaos purred loudly, probably liking the sound of that.

"Then," Sean said, getting more excited, "we could build a giant slide from our house right into the village. It would be the fastest way to get around, and so much fun!"

He laughed, imagining sliding down a huge slide every morning. "We could even make it a water slide in the summer. The kids in the village would love it!"

Chaos looked at him, tilting his head as if wondering how a cat could use a slide.

"And what about a party?" Sean continued. "We could throw the biggest, silliest party Limeridge has ever seen! There would be clowns, balloons, and a cake as big as a house. We could even have a magician - though I bet none of them could do tricks as good as the ones you do with your paws, Chaos!"

Chaos meowed again, and Sean took it as a sign that Chaos approved of the party idea.

"We could even travel," Sean mused, looking up at the sky. "Imagine us, traveling the world. We could see pyramids, jungles, and big cities! You could have a little cat passport with your photo in it!"

Chaos seemed to like this idea too. He started walking with a little more swagger, like a cat ready to see the world.

Sean's ideas got sillier and sillier as they walked. "Maybe we could even buy a spaceship and go to the moon! I wonder if they have cheese there, like in the cartoons. We could have a picnic on the moon!"

Chaos looked at Sean as if he was saying, "Now you're being really silly."

But that was the fun of it. Sean and Chaos were on an adventure, not just in the forest, but in their imaginations too. They laughed and explored, dreaming up all sorts of wild and wonderful things to do with a pot of gold. It was a day filled with hope, laughter, and the joy of imagining what could be.

After wandering through the forest, having lots of fun and laughs, Sean and his cat Chaos finally found something incredible. They came to a place in the forest where everything seemed extra bright and cheerful. The clovers on the ground were so green they looked like they were glowing. It was like they had walked into a part of the forest from a fairy tale.

And there, right where the rainbow seemed to touch the ground, was a pot. But it wasn't just any pot. It was the pot of gold they had been joking about! It was shining and sparkling, full of gold coins that glittered in the sunlight.

Sean's eyes got so wide, they looked like they might pop out of his head. His mouth dropped open, and for a moment, he couldn't say a word. He just pointed at the pot, looking back and forth between it and Chaos.

"Chaos, look!" he finally blurted out. "The gold! It's real! We actually found it!"

Chaos meowed loudly, his tail swishing back and forth quickly. He seemed just as surprised as Sean.

Sean started hopping around like a rabbit, too excited to stand still. "I can't believe it! We're rich, Chaos! Rich! We can buy a mountain of cat treats, build the biggest slide, and have the silliest party ever!"

He laughed and danced around the pot, his glasses slipping down his nose in all the excitement. He had to push them back up every few seconds, but he was too happy to care.

"Imagine that, a real pot of gold at the end of a rainbow. Who would have thought? This is the best day ever!"

Chaos, being a cat, was more interested in the shiny pot than the gold itself. He walked around it, sniffing and giving it a few curious paws.

Sean sat down next to the pot, still not believing his luck. He picked up a gold coin and held it up to the light, watching it sparkle.

"We did it, Chaos! We found the treasure! This is going to be a story to tell everyone in Limeridge. They won't believe it!"

Right next to the pot of gold, almost like he had popped out of a storybook, stood a leprechaun. He was a small, mischievous-looking fellow, with a green hat and a bright red beard that seemed to have its own personality.

The leprechaun was watching Sean and Chaos with a twinkle in his eye. It was like he was trying not to laugh at how surprised and excited they were. His eyes were full of fun and secrets, like he knew all the stories of the forest and then some.

As Sean danced around and Chaos sniffed the pot, the leprechaun just leaned against a tree, arms crossed, with a grin on his face. He looked like he was enjoying a private joke. Every now and then, he'd wink or give a little nod, as if he was saying, "Yep, you found it, but there's more to this story!"

When Sean finally noticed the leprechaun, he stopped mid-dance and stared, his mouth open again. "A real leprechaun!" he exclaimed. "This day just keeps getting better and better!"

The leprechaun gave a little bow and said, "Well now, you've found my pot of gold. Quite the adventure you've had, eh?"

His voice was playful, and he had a cheeky smile that made Sean laugh. "I thought leprechauns were just in stories," Sean said.

"Oh, we're very real," the leprechaun replied, winking. "Just like this pot of gold.

Chaos meowed, looking up at the leprechaun as if he understood every word.

The leprechaun's expression was full of mirth and mystery. He looked like he could burst into laughter or disappear in a puff of smoke at any moment. He was like a character from one of Sean's wild tales, full of charm and surprises.

As Sean and Chaos stood there with the leprechaun, the forest seemed even more magical. It was like they had stepped into a world where anything could happen, they prepared themselves to navigate the delightful pathways of wonder, mystery, and the heartwarming narratives of life's magical symphony. The forest, with its ethereal beauty and mystical presence, stood as a witness to their journey, celebrating the spirit of exploration and the joy of life's enchanting tales.

Chapter 5

The Leprechaun's Lament and Sean's Triumph

"Hey, big foot!" chuckled the leprechaun, pointing at Sean's shoes. His voice bubbled like soda pop. "Stumbled upon my secret stash, have you?" He wiggled his itty-bitty fingers towards a pot that shone like a golden sun. But this was no ordinary pot. Oh no! It was like a circus of luck, juggling joy, sadness, and a gazillion goofy surprises!

Sean, still beaming with excitement, turned to the leprechaun, and said, "Well, now that we've found this pot of gold, it's ours, right? I've got so many plans for it!"

The leprechaun, with a sly smile, raised his hand and replied, "Hold on there, laddie. It's not that simple."

Sean, a bit puzzled, adjusted his glasses and asked, "What do you mean? We found the gold fair and square."

Sean was trying to understand what the leprechaun was saying about the pot of gold. The leprechaun, with a twinkle in his eye, did a funny little dance, hopping and skipping around the pot.

"This isn't just a bunch of gold coins, Sean," the leprechaun said, still dancing. "Think of it more like a magical movie theater. Each gold coin is like a ticket to a wild and crazy story!"

He then added with a laugh, "It's like a rollercoaster that doesn't just go up and down, but twists and turns through a world of laughter and surprises!"

Sean looked at the pot, his eyes wide. He scratched his head, which was getting all muddled with these funny ideas. "So, this pot is like a circus full of magic and tricks?" he asked. He started to imagine what that would be like.

In his mind, he dived into the pot of gold, like diving into a pool. But instead of water, it was a sparkling cascade of gold coins. He imagined himself swimming through this golden waterfall and landing in a world that was completely topsy-turvy.

In this silly world, cats wore top hats and monocles, strutting around like little gentlemen. Shoes didn't just sit quietly on feet; they tapped and danced, putting on their own little musical shows. And the air – it smelled like popcorn and candy, making Sean's mouth water.

Sean pictured trees with leaves that giggled when the wind blew, and flowers that sang in harmony. The sky was a canvas of swirling colors, like someone had taken a paintbrush and swirled all the colors of the rainbow together.

He imagined Chaos, his cat, riding a tiny bicycle, meowing in tune to some jazzy tune. And instead of birds, there were flying cupcakes, zooming through the air with a trail of glitter.

Sean laughed at the thought, his laughter echoing through the forest. "That sounds amazing!" he said to the leprechaun. "A magical, giggly, topsy-turvy world!"

The leprechaun nodded, still dancing. "That's the spirit, Sean! This pot of gold is your ticket to a world where anything is possible, and every day is a new adventure!"

Sean's imagination was running wild with all the fun and crazy things he could do with a magical pot of gold. It was like stepping into a story where he was the main character, and every turn was a new and exciting page.

The leprechaun, who looked like he might be getting a bit peckish or just wanted to take a break, gave his shoulders a little jazzy shrug. "Go ahead, take the pot if you're ready to deal with all the twists and turns of fate!" he said with a playful grin. "But be ready, Sean. It's going to be a wild ride, like a rollercoaster through a tunnel of luck and laughter!"

With those words, the leprechaun started to disappear, blending back into the magic of the forest, like he was part of an old fairytale coming to life.

Sean looked down at the pot of gold in his hands. He held it as carefully as if it was a big, delicious birthday cake. He felt like he was at the start of a brand new story, one filled with bouncing tales and adventures as colorful as rainbows.

With every step Sean took, it was like he could hear the crackle of wild, untold stories in the pot. He imagined the gold coins inside were not just coins, but little boxes of surprises, ready to pop open like jack-in-the-boxes. Each one would jump out with a new, crazy adventure.

"Who knows what will happen next?" Sean thought to himself, excited. "Maybe I'll meet talking animals, or find a tree that grows candy instead of fruit!"

He imagined walking through a forest where the leaves played music, and rivers flowed with lemonade. In his mind, clouds were fluffy like cotton candy, and stars winked at him, sharing their own secret stories.

As he walked back through the forest with Chaos, his steps felt lighter, like he was walking on a path made of clouds. He couldn't wait to tell everyone in Limeridge about the magical pot and all the adventures that were waiting for them.

"Get ready, Limeridge," he said out loud, "we're about to have some fun that's out of this world!"

And with that, Sean, carrying his magical pot of gold, and Chaos, his faithful sidekick, headed back into the village, ready for whatever crazy, wonderful stories were about to unfold. The air seemed to buzz with excitement, and even Chaos's tail twitched with anticipation. It was going to be an adventure they'd never forget.

Chapter 6

A Frogtastic Fandango

Sean held the magical pot of gold tightly in his arms, feeling as lucky as a kid with a mountain of ice cream cones. He hummed a happy tune, ready to skip back home through Murphy's Forest, thinking of all the fun times the gold would bring. But the leprechaun's pot had other plans, plans as wacky as a chicken playing the trumpet!

Sean was strolling happily through Murphy's Forest, his mind filled with dreams as sweet as candy. He imagined the sky full of fluffy clouds made of cotton candy and raindrops of chocolate cookies tumbling down softly. But, as he floated in his scrumptiously sweet daydreams, the sky began to grumble and groan like a hungry tummy.

Just as Sean and Chaos were making their way back, the sky put on its own show. Suddenly, there was a bright flash of lightning, like the world's biggest camera taking a picture. Then came the thunder, roaring and rumbling like a giant lion in the jungle. It was so loud that Sean jumped, and even Chaos's ears twitched.

Sean looked up, half-expecting to get soaked by raindrops. But instead of rain, something totally unexpected happened. Plop! Right on top of Sean's head landed a frog. Yep, a frog! A little green one, looking just as shocked to be there as Sean was to have it on his head.

Sean's eyes went wide, and he let out a surprised yelp. The frog, meanwhile, just sat there on his head, blinking its big, round eyes as if it was saying, "Oops, wrong stop!"

Chaos looked up at the frog and meowed, his tail swishing in curiosity. He seemed to wonder how this little green visitor had just dropped from the sky.

Sean, trying to stay still, said, "Well, hello there, Mr. Frog. Fancy meeting you here, on my head!"

The frog just ribbited, as if it was saying hello back.

Then Sean chuckled and gently picked the frog off his head, holding it in his hands. "You're quite the skydiver, aren't you?" he joked.

The frog looked at Sean and then at Chaos, its eyes wide and curious. It seemed to be okay, just a bit surprised by its sudden journey from the sky to Sean's head.

"I guess we have our first adventure already, Chaos," Sean said with a laugh. "Our pot of gold is bringing us friends from the sky!"

Chaos meowed and nudged the frog gently with his nose, like he was welcoming it to their adventure.

Sean's eyes twinkled. "Mr. Frog, will you join us back home" he said.

But before Sean could get an answer, the sky decided it was party time! The air filled with a whirlwind of whirling, twirling frogs. It was a froggy fiesta! Frogs here, frogs there, frogs everywhere—ribbit-ribbiting as they spiraled down from the sky like wacky, green snowflakes.

Sean's mouth dropped open in awe. "Oh, froggy rain, this is totally bananas!" he laughed. His new frog friends bounced on his head, wiggled on his shoulders, and some even performed funny somersaults in mid-air, landing softly in the magical pot of gold.

The forest became a fabulous froggy festival. Each leaf on the trees seemed to giggle, each flower seemed to sway in delight, and even the wind seemed to whistle a happy, hopping tune. Sean danced and twirled, joining the jolly jumping jamboree, turning the forest path into a hopping hilarious runway of ribbits and rolls.

With his heart filled with giggles and his pot of gold now a bouncy castle of frogs, Sean continued his wonderfully wacky walk-through Murphy's Forest, ready for more surprising and silly sky surprises.

The world around Sean turned into a circus of silly surprises. Every step he took, there was a hop, a skip, and a froggy jump! Even the trees seemed to laugh, their leaves rustling and clapping in joy at the playful parade.

Sean decided to go along with the giggles and grins. "If the sky gives you frogs, let's make it a hopping party!" he said, putting on a hat of happiness and joining the ribbiting revelry.

As he trotted down the path, each footstep turned into a funny frolic. Frogs played leapfrog over his shoes, and some even tried to high-five him with their tiny, webbed hands. It seemed like the pot of gold had turned the day into a playground of pranks and playfulness.

People in Limeridge watched in awe and amusement. They giggled, clapped, and cheered at the hopping hilarity happening before their eyes. The once ordinary and quiet town buzzed and bubbled with laughter and lovable lunacy.

Sean's journey became a treasure chest of chuckles and cheers, each moment more magical and merrier than the last. With a heart full of happiness and a pot full of playful luck (and a few jumpy frogs), Sean's adventure became a legendary tale of laughter and loveable looniness, a story that would tickle the town's funny bone for ages to come.

So, with froggy friends and a pot of unpredictable surprises, Sean's journey turned into a carnival of curiosity and joy, making the day as delightful as a bathtub filled with rubber duckies!

Chapter 7

Limeridge's New Adventure

After the unexpected froggy encounter, Sean was bubbling with excitement to share his adventure with everyone in Limeridge. He gathered all the townspeople in the village square. The people of Limeridge, curious about Sean's latest escapade, formed a big circle around him.

"Listen up, everyone!" Sean began, his voice full of excitement. "I've got the most amazing story to tell you!"

One of the villagers, Mrs. Jenkins, who was known for her love of gossip, leaned in, and asked, "What is it this time, Sean? Did you find a treasure chest?"

Sean grinned and said, "Even better! I found a magical pot of gold in Murphy's Forest!"

Old Mr. Thompson, who was sitting on a bench with his dog, chuckled. "A pot of gold, you say?, Did a rainbow lead you there?"

"Yes, exactly!" Sean replied. "And there was a leprechaun too!"

The crowd murmured with surprise and skepticism. Leprechauns were stuff of fairy tales, after all.

Little Timmy, one of the village kids, tugged on Sean's sleeve. "Did the leprechaun grant you wishes?" he asked with wide eyes.

Sean laughed and ruffled Timmy's hair. "No wishes, Timmy, but the leprechaun told me the gold is magical. It's meant to bring joy and help others!"

Mrs. Green, the local baker, smiled warmly. "So, what are you planning to do with this magical gold, Sean?"

Sean's eyes sparkled with ideas. "I'm thinking of using it to make Limeridge the happiest place ever! Maybe we can fix up the park, or throw a big festival for everyone!"

The crowd started to buzz with excitement. The idea of using the gold for the town was something everyone could get excited about.

Mr. Thompson, still a bit doubtful, asked, "And how do we know this gold is truly magical?"

Sean, full of confidence, replied, "Well, Mr. Thompson, let's just say that on my way here, a frog fell from the sky right onto my head!"

The crowd erupted in laughter, picturing the always-surprising Sean with a frog on his head.

"Only Sean could have such an adventure," Mrs. Jenkins said, shaking her head but smiling.

The people of Limeridge, now buzzing with excitement and laughter, started to share their own ideas for the magical gold. Children talked about new playground equipment, while the adults thought of ways to beautify the village.

As the sun set over Limeridge, the village square was filled with laughter and chatter. Sean's story of magical gold, a leprechaun, and a sky-diving frog had brought a new sense of wonder and excitement to the town. And just like that, Sean's adventure turned into a new chapter of joy and possibilities for everyone in Limeridge.

Chapter 8

Pickle Party Palace

Sean, who was always ready for a new surprise, woke up one regular morning. The sun was shining, the birds were singing, and the clock was cheerfully ticking away, announcing the start of another day. But then, something unexpected happened. There was a series of rapid, loud doorbell rings, like someone was playing a tune with the doorbell.

"Who could that be so early in the morning?" Sean wondered, rubbing the sleep from his eyes. He stumbled out of bed, still in his pajamas, which had funny pictures of cats riding bicycles.

As he made his way to the door, the doorbell kept ringing in a funny pattern. "Ding-dong, ding-ding-dong," it went, making Sean chuckle. "Someone's in a hurry!"

He opened the door, and there stood a man with a very serious face, like he never smiled in his life. He looked as strict as a school principal on the first day of school.

But what really caught Sean's attention was what was behind the serious man. There was a huge pile of boxes, so many that they seemed to touch the clouds! And these weren't just any boxes. They were decorated with pictures of pickles – not ordinary pickles, but dancing pickles wearing tiny, funky sunglasses. The pickles looked like they were having a party on the boxes.

Sean's eyes went wide with surprise. "Wow, that's a lot of boxes! And with dancing pickles, no less!" he said with a laugh.

“Congratulations!” the man announced in a voice as grand as a game show hosts. “You, Sean, are the lucky winner of our fabulous lottery!”

Sean's eyes widened, and his heart started to beat like a happy drum. A lottery! Visions of a mountain of gold coins, fancy cars, and a house as big as a castle flooded his imagination. Without waiting for another word, he started hopping up and down like a kangaroo on a trampoline. "Wow, a lottery!" he cheered.

The man tried to continue, waving his hands to get Sean's attention. "Wait, there's more," he said. But Sean was too lost in his jumps and joyful whoops to listen.

Finally, the man took a deep breath, gathered all the volume his lungs could muster, and shouted, "You've won a lifetime supply of PICKLES! Yes, that's right, pickles!"

Sean froze mid-air, his dreams of riches popped like a bubble. He landed back on the ground with a thud, his mind trying to wrap around the word - pickles. A lifetime supply of the tangy, green things? His house now the kingdom of pickles?

He looked at the boxes, each one promising an eternity of pickle-powered meals. Breakfast, lunch, dinner, all with the starring guest: the crunchy pickles. The man at the door tried to keep a straight face, maybe wondering if Sean would start jumping again or possibly burst into tears.

Sean smiled, still absorbing his curious prize. A world of pickles awaited him, a tangy adventure in every box. His life had just turned into a funny pickle story, a tale sprinkled with the zesty surprises of the universe's sense of humor.

As Sean was still trying digest the news, the serious man handed him a card. The card was as colorful as the boxes, with more pictures of those funky dancing pickles on it.

"If you ever finish all these," the man said in his serious, no-nonsense voice, "just give us a call. We'll be happy to deliver another load. Remember, it's a lifetime supply of pickles."

Sean, now holding the card and still wearing the pickle costume, burst out laughing. "A lifetime supply of pickles? That's a lot of pickles!"

The man nodded, still serious. "Yes, sir. Pickles for life. Enjoy." And with that, he turned and walked away, leaving Sean standing there, surrounded by pickle paraphernalia.

Sean looked at Chaos, who was still wearing the tiny pickle sunglasses. "Did you hear that, Chaos? We've got pickles for life! I guess we're going to be the pickle capital of Limeridge!"

This strange prize left Sean scratching his head in disbelief. Ironically, pickles were not among his preferred tastes. He found them to be an odd, sour presence that seemed to play quirky games with one's taste buds.

The arrival of this enormous pickle consignment transformed Sean's home. Every conceivable space seemed to have been invaded by jars of these green, curious entities. They made their presence felt in the most unlikely places, turning the house into a bizarre exhibition of their pervasive existence.

The news of Sean's unusual windfall spread across the town, evoking reactions ranging from amusement to curious wonder. Sean's house became an epicenter of this newfound fascination, with the townspeople engaging in whispers and chuckles, discussing the strange and overwhelming pickle invasion.

Despite the overwhelming pickle presence, Sean decided to turn this unexpected situation into an opportunity for communal joy. He opened his doors, offering free pickles to everyone, turning his house into a unique hub of sharing and lightheartedness.

The townspeople responded with laughter and gratitude, participating in this unusual celebration of generosity. Sean's home transformed into a lively venue, where the ordinary rhythms of life were temporarily replaced by the strange yet joyful carnival revolving around pickles.

As the days went by in Limeridge, Sean's house had turned into a pickle palace, and it seemed like every corner had its own surprise. Pickles had become a part of his everyday life in the funniest ways.

One morning, Sean opened the fridge to get some milk, and guess what? A pile of pickles fell out! They bounced around the kitchen floor like green, bouncy balls. Sean just laughed and tried to catch them, while Chaos watched, amused and a bit confused.

Then, there was the time Sean wanted to sit down and read his newspaper. He flopped down on the sofa, only to land on a pickle. The pickle let out such a funny sound that Sean couldn't help but burst into laughter. Chaos jumped on the sofa, pouncing on the pickle, making it squeak even more.

Even doing laundry became a pickle adventure. Sean opened the washing machine, and out tumbled a couple of pickles in the socks. "Well, these will be perfect for the pickle parade!" he thought, chuckling to himself.

When he went to bed, he found pickle on his lampshade, casting funny pickle-shaped shadows on the wall. Sean lay in bed, looking at the dancing pickle shadows, and couldn't help but smile. Even his dreams started to have pickles in them!

Every day was filled with these quirky, pickle-related discoveries. It was like living in a comedy show where pickles were the main characters. Sean never knew when or where the next pickle surprise would pop up. It made every day interesting and full of laughter.

His friends in Limeridge started to joke that Sean's house was the 'Pickle Museum.' It was all very silly, but it brought so much fun and joy, not just to Sean and Chaos, but to everyone in Limeridge.

Despite the overwhelming pickle presence, Sean maintained a spirit of humor and acceptance. He allowed this strange chapter to unfold with as much grace and lightheartedness as possible, remaining receptive to the unpredictable nature of life's offerings.

In the heart of this unusual narrative, Sean found himself navigating a landscape marked by randomness and unexpected developments. His home, once familiar and predictable, had transformed into a dynamic stage where the unexpected had become a constant guest. Even as he lived amidst an overflow of pickles, Sean held on to a sense of hope and readiness to embrace the next set of surprises that life would inevitably present.

Life with a lifetime supply of pickles was never boring. In fact, it was full of laughter, surprises, and, of course, lots and lots of pickles. Sean never knew what pickle adventure awaited him each day, and that was the best part.

Through this experience, the town of Limeridge also participated in a unique tale of shared stories and communal participation. The pickle saga became a temporary yet memorable chapter in the town's collective memory, leaving behind traces of laughter, curiosity, and the lingering essence of life's unpredictable surprises.

Chapter 9

Marching Band Madness

Sean, an adventurer at heart with a home oddly filled with pickles, was nestled comfortably on his sofa, attempting to immerse himself in the embrace of a peaceful evening. He had planned a quiet night, hoping it would unfold with the gentleness and simplicity of a calming melody.

That evening, as Sean was relaxing, thinking it would be just another quiet night in his pickle-filled house, but as fate would have it, the universe had a different, comical plan for Sean's evening. Suddenly, there was a loud, rousing sound, like a whole marching band had decided to set up right outside his door. It was a cacophony of trumpets, drums, and tubas, all playing in a lively, upbeat rhythm.

Startled, Sean jumped up from his chair, his eyes as wide as saucers. "What in the world of dancing pickles is that?" he exclaimed.

Chaos, who had been dozing off, woke up with a jolt. His cat ears perked up, and he looked as puzzled as Sean felt.

With a mix of surprise and curiosity, Sean tiptoed to the door. He felt like a detective about to solve a mystery. He slowly turned the doorknob, opened the door, and whoosh! In marched a band, bright and bouncy as a parade of peacocks! There were tuba players huffing and puffing like tired dragons, and their tubas belched out tunes as round and heavy as bowling balls. Drummers drummed with the enthusiasm of woodpeckers in a forest of juicy bugs. Their drums rattled and echoed, turning Sean's quiet room into a jungle of jumpy rhythms.

A fellow with a trumpet blasted notes as high and wobbly as a circus tightrope, and a trombonist slid his slide so vigorously it seemed to dance the cha-cha-cha on its own! The flute players fluttered their fingers over their instruments, conjuring a windstorm of whirling, twirling melodies.

Sean tried to speak, to ask them what the pickles was going on, but his words drowned in this ocean of uproarious sounds. The band played on, unstoppable as a runaway train on a track of tunes.

Sean: Hey! What's all this ruckus? Is it Saint Patrick's Day already or is my calendar playing pranks on me?

Band Leader: (Nods at Sean, and then blows into his trumpet like a playful elephant announcing the start of a jungle party.)

Sean: (Trying to be heard over the blaring of tubas and the clash of cymbals) Excuse me! EX-CUSE ME! What brings this musical hurricane into my living room?

Drummer: (Bashes the drums even harder, creating a rhythm like a herd of galloping giraffes, while giving Sean a big, cheeky grin.)

Sean: (Almost pleading now, his words jiving with the jazzy tunes) Seriously, folks! Can someone hit the pause button? I can't hear myself think over this symphony of sound explosions!

Trumpeter: (Takes a deep breath and sends a cascade of notes flying around the room, each one popping like a mischievous firecracker.)

Sean: (Laughing in disbelief) You guys sure know how to make some joyous noise, but can we turn the volume knob down a little? We're not trying to wake up the entire neighborhood, are we?

Trombonist: (Slides into a deep, belly-laughing note that booms around the room like a bouncy ball on a caffeine rush.)

Sean: Okay, okay! Let's make a deal! (Pauses, hoping for a musical intermission.) How about we swap the grand orchestra vibes for a pocket-sized melody? Maybe a soft serenade instead of a triumphant parade?

Flutist: (Replies with a flurry of notes, fluttering through the air like a flock of pigeons who've found a loaf of bread on a sidewalk.)

Sean: (Laughing, surrendering to the joyful chaos) Alright! Go on then! Play your heart out! Let's turn this room into a stage of unstoppable tunes and celebrate the magic of melodies running wild!

It seemed like the universe had twisted the radio dial, and instead of a soft evening of relaxation, Sean got a booming, banging, tooting, hooting concert in his living room. Sean's peaceful night was packed away in a trumpet case, and the band played on, filling his room with musical mayhem and hilarious haphazard harmonies!

Seeking an escape from the overpowering concert, Sean decided to step outside, hoping the absence of an audience would encourage the band to cease their enthusiastic performance. But life had another surprise in its vast repertoire of unexpected events. The band, dedicated to their lively procession, accompanied Sean outdoors, filling the open spaces with their echoing, joyous tunes.

Limeridge became a spontaneous stage, and the townspeople, the unexpected audience to a parade of sound and celebration. They witnessed the march with eyes wide in wonder, sharing smiles and laughter as the music and spectacle unraveled through their streets. They found humor and delight in the unanticipated concert, the music infusing the town with an air of liveliness and joy.

As the band continued their auditory journey through the town, it seemed as though the very streets and buildings resonated with their rhythmic beats. The ordinary surroundings were painted with extraordinary colors by the music's lively strokes. Each note seemed to weave stories in the air, narrating tales of spontaneity and vibrant surprises.

People emerged from their homes, drawn by the magnetic pull of the music. They became willing participants in this unexpected festivity, their hearts and feet tapping along to the irresistible rhythms. Each member of the community shared in the laughter and joy, contributing to the collective atmosphere of celebration.

Sean, despite initially seeking peace and quiet, became the centerpiece of this unfolding mural of melodies. The music seemed to follow him, composing a soundtrack that echoed through every corner of Limeridge. The adventure of the evening was captured in each note, creating memories imprinted with melodies and echoes of shared joy.

After three whole hours of lively, toe-tapping music, the marching band finally came to a stop. The whole time, they played all sorts of fun tunes, from jazzy numbers to fast-paced marches. Sean, along with his cat Chaos and all the neighbors, had been enjoying the show, clapping and dancing along.

After three hours of toe-tapping, lively music that had filled the neighborhood with an air of festivity, the marching band finally stopped playing. The whole street had come alive with their tunes, drawing people out of their houses to enjoy the unexpected concert. Sean, surrounded by his amused and slightly bewildered neighbors, approached the band leader, a tall man with a bright red uniform and a hat that looked like it belonged in a parade.

"Excuse me," Sean called out, his curiosity getting the better of him. "That was fantastic, but I've got to ask, why did you choose my house for your concert?"

The band leader, wiping sweat from his brow with a handkerchief that matched his uniform, turned to Sean with a smile. "Well, sir, we received a note with a gold coin in it, instructing us to play for Sean O'Reilly of Limeridge for three hours. And here we are!"

Sean's mouth fell open in surprise. "A gold coin? From my pot?"

"It was a gold coin, we don't know from where," the band leader said, smiling. "It's not every day we get such an unusual payment."

Puzzled, Sean thanked the band leader and watched as the band members, still buzzing with the energy of their performance, began to pack up their instruments and chat among themselves about the evening's unique experience.

As the band marched away, leaving behind a street full of excited chatter and laughter, Sean turned to his house, deep in thought. The magical pot of gold – he hadn't thought much about it since the day he found it, except when it brought him surprise guests like the marching band.

He entered his house, where Chaos, his cat, was lounging comfortably, having enjoyed the evening's entertainment from the window. Sean headed straight for the place where he kept the magical pot of gold. Sure enough, the lid was ajar, and one coin was missing.

Sean remembered the day he found the pot of gold, how the leprechaun had warned him about its magic. "Be careful with these coins," the leprechaun had said. "They're not your ordinary gold. They hold magic that can bring both joy and surprise."

"Looks like the leprechaun wasn't kidding," Sean mused to himself. The idea that the coins could somehow be used without him knowing was both exciting and a little unsettling.

As he stood there, looking at the pot, he thought back to all the strange and wonderful things that had happened since he found it. The frog from the sky, the lifetime supply of pickles, and now a marching band appearing at his doorstep.

He wondered if perhaps the coins had a mind of their own, or if someone else knew about them and was using them for these surprises. The mystery deepened, and Sean felt like he was in one of those detective stories he loved to read.

The next morning, Sean decided to do a little investigating. He went around the neighborhood, asking if anyone had seen anything unusual the day the marching band showed up. Most of his neighbors just laughed, thinking Sean was up to his usual whimsical antics.

Mrs. Jenkins, who lived two doors down and was known for her nosiness, said, "Well, I did see a strange man walking around the day before. He was carrying a big envelope and looking at the houses like he was searching for something."

"That could be our mysterious gold coin spender," Sean thought, his curiosity piqued.

He thanked Mrs. Jenkins and continued his informal investigation, but no one else had seen anything out of the ordinary. It seemed the mystery of the gold coin user would remain unsolved for now.

That evening, as Sean sat in his living room, he thought about the magic of the coins. "Maybe it's not about figuring out how they work, but just enjoying the surprises they bring," he said to Chaos, who was curled up on his lap.

Just then, there was a knock on the door. Sean got up to answer it, half-expecting another surprise guest. But it was just the mailman, delivering a package.

As the days passed, Sean found himself encountering more surprises. One bright morning, Sean stumbled out of bed, still half-asleep, and shuffled to the mailbox. To his surprise, he found a package addressed to him. Inside was a stack of comic books, his absolute favorite series! There was a note attached that read, "Enjoy a year of adventures, courtesy of a mysterious benefactor!" Sean's eyes lit up like Christmas lights. "A whole year of comics? This is like winning the lottery!" he exclaimed.

Chaos, who was always by Sean's side, looked at the comics with mild interest before going back to chasing his tail.

The surprises didn't stop there. A few days later, Sean came home from a walk with Chaos to find a brand-new garden bench sitting on his lawn. It was a beautiful bench, painted bright blue with little yellow sunflowers on it. Attached to it was a simple note: “Enjoy the view, from a friend.”

Sean sat on the bench, slightly bemused. "Well, Chaos, now we have the best seat in the house for bird watching," he said. Chaos jumped up beside him, looking quite pleased with this new addition to their garden.

The neighbors started to talk about the mysterious happenings at Sean's house. Mrs. Jenkins, who could always be counted on for a good piece of gossip, said to her friend, "You never know what you'll find at Sean's place. It's better than watching television!"

Each surprise brought a smile to Sean’s face and added a bit of excitement to his life. He started to look forward to these unexpected gifts, wondering what each new day would bring.

His neighbors began to get in on the fun too, often stopping by to see what new and bizarre thing had appeared in Sean’s life. Sean’s house became a place of laughter and wonder, a little beacon of joy in Limeridge.

And as for the magical pot of gold, Sean treated it with a new respect, aware of its power to bring joy in the most unexpected ways. He no longer tried to solve the mystery of the gold coins but instead embraced the magic and surprises they brought into his life.

Chapter 10

Duck Duck, Quack Quack, Sean!

In Limeridge, where oddities were now as common as morning dew, a curious spectacle unfolded on an ordinary afternoon. Sean, familiar with bizarre happenings, decided to embrace the day's gentle embrace by visiting the park, expecting nothing more than the usual company of ducks and the soft rustling of trees. The universe, however, had orchestrated an extraordinary performance that was about to unravel its comedic curtains just for him.

As Sean stepped into the park, he was greeted by a scene that was straight out of a storybook. The park in Limeridge was always a picturesque place, but today, it felt even more magical. The vibrant path was lined with a kaleidoscope of flowers, blooming in brilliant hues of reds, yellows, blues, and purples. The air was fragrant with the sweet aroma of blossoms, and the gentle hum of busy bees added to the park's tranquil melody.

The sun was shining brightly, casting dappled shadows through the leaves of the tall, majestic trees that swayed gently in the breeze. The grass was a perfect shade of green, looking like a soft carpet inviting visitors to sit down and relax.

As Sean walked further into the park, he noticed the little details that made this place special. The flowerbeds were meticulously cared for, with each flower seeming to smile up at him. The birds were singing cheerfully, flitting from branch to branch in the trees overhead. A nearby fountain bubbled and gurgled, its water sparkling in the sunlight, adding a soothing soundtrack to the peaceful surroundings.

Then, something unusual happened. The ordinary ducks of the park, usually so calm and collected, suddenly burst into action. It was as if they had been waiting just for Sean. They flocked around him, quacking and flapping their wings with excitement. To Sean, it looked like they were putting on a performance just for him.

The ducks, with their glossy feathers and proud orange beaks, paraded around Sean as if he were a celebrity. They waddled in circles, flapping their wings and tilting their heads, looking up at him as if he were the grand marshal of their parade.

Sean couldn't help but burst into laughter at this unexpected welcome. "Well, hello there!" he greeted them. The ducks seemed to respond with even more enthusiastic quacking.

Chaos, perched on Sean's shoulder, was equally amused and slightly baffled by the ducks' behavior. He meowed inquisitively, watching the feathery spectacle with wide, curious eyes.

People in the park paused to witness this delightful scene. Children giggled and pointed, while their parents took out their phones to capture the moment. It was like a scene from a whimsical movie, with Sean and his entourage of ducks taking center stage.

The ducks escorted Sean past the beds of flowers, their petals gently swaying in the breeze. They followed him along the winding path, past the fountain where the water danced in the sunlight. Even the squirrels seemed to stop and take notice, pausing in their playful chases to see what the fuss was about.

Caught in the middle of this unexpected duck carnival, Sean found himself right in the center of a feathery, quacky whirlwind. The park, usually a haven of peace and quiet, had transformed into a noisy, lively spectacle. Everywhere Sean looked, there were ducks. They quacked, they flapped, and they waddled after him as if he were the pied piper of Limeridge.

As Sean walked, trying to enjoy his usual peaceful stroll, the ducks followed him with what seemed like unwavering dedication. Their wings flapped in unison, creating a sound that was part fanfare, part comedy. Their little feet waddled in rhythm, turning their procession into a sort of synchronized dance that echoed through the park.

Sean couldn't help but laugh at the absurdity of it all. "Well, this isn't the quiet morning I had in mind," he said to Chaos, who was perched on his shoulder, looking as bemused as Sean felt.

Seeking some tranquility, Sean quickened his pace, winding through paths bordered by lush green bushes and vibrant flowers. But the ducks were undeterred. They kept up with him, their waddling turning into a comical chase. People in the park stopped to watch, their laughter joining the chorus of quacks.

It was like a scene from a slapstick comedy. Sean, followed by a parade of ducks, dashed past rose bushes in full bloom, under the shade of towering oak trees, and around the sparkling fountain. The ducks were relentless in their pursuit, their quacks filling the air with a humorous soundtrack.

Every time Sean thought he had lost them, he would turn a corner and find them right behind him, as dedicated as ever. It was as if they had decided that Sean was their new leader, and they were his loyal followers.

Trying to outpace the ducks, Sean zigzagged across the park's grassy expanses, between benches where people sat with their morning coffee, and alongside the small pond where the ducks usually spent their time. But no matter where he went, the ducks were right there, waddling after him with enthusiasm.

Witnesses of this unusual event were swept by waves of laughter. Their eyes widened in disbelief as they became the audience of this spontaneous performance. The world seemed to sway along with the ducks' wacky waltz, as the earth itself became a laughing spectator in this extraordinary play.

Sean found himself in a wacky race in the garden, chased by a quacking crowd of ducks. They were his crazy fans, flapping and quacking like they were at a rock concert! Sean tried every move - ducking under branches and zig-zagging past flowers that seemed to be in on the joke, giggling in full bloom.

But no luck! The ducks were like super fans, not giving up, turning the whole place into a funny, quacky musical.

Their beaks were like instruments, playing a noisy, happy tune that filled the air, making everything feel like a big, silly party. It was like the garden had turned into a wild, wacky art piece, all thanks to Sean's funny, feathered followers!

Sean's walk in the park turned into a goofy, duck-filled adventure! Imagine him, dancing and dodging like a clown in big shoes, trying to outstep the quacking crew of fluffy comedians waddling behind. Each step Sean took, the ducks copied, turning the pathway into a comedy stage. People all around stopped to watch the hilarious show, giggling and whispering, making the park feel like a giant, laughing theater.

It wasn't just a walk; it was a crazy duck parade! Quacks, footsteps, and chuckles mixed together in the air, creating a funny music that played as the soundtrack of this loony tune. Everyone watched as Sean and the ducks performed their wild and wacky dance, turning an ordinary day into a laugh-out-loud duck drama!

Sean had reached his funny breaking point! "No more ducky follies," he decided, lacing up his imaginary superhero boots. Off he zoomed, like a rocket on roller skates, leaving a trail of dust and chuckles behind! The ducks, not wanting to miss the running party, turned into feathery, flapping racers. Quacking like honking cars in a traffic jam, they waddled, raced, and flapped, trying to keep up with Speedy Sean!

The park became their loony racetrack: Sean darting like a pinball, the ducks bouncing after him like fluffy rubber balls! Over bridges, through bushes, zigzagging like a cartoon chase - their funny feet turned the place into a playground of giggles and waddles!

Sean's legs became swirling tornadoes, zipping through every nook and cranny of the park! Trees whispered, flowers giggled, and the paths became whirlwinds of wacky chase music.!

Finally, Sean stopped, out of breath from the unexpected exercise. The ducks gathered around him, still quacking and flapping, but now with a sense of accomplishment, as if they had completed an important mission.

Sean sat down on a nearby bench, the ducks settling around him, some even daring to hop up onto the bench next to him. Chaos jumped down from Sean's shoulder, cautiously eyeing his new feathery companions.

"Well, I guess this is my life now," Sean said, chuckling as he petted one of the ducks. "Leader of the duck parade in Limeridge."

The people in the park continued to watch and laugh, enjoying the unusual spectacle. Children pointed and clapped, delighted by the ducks' antics.

As the sun climbed higher in the sky, the ducks finally began to disperse, returning to their usual spots in the park. Sean, still smiling, got up from the bench. He looked around at the peaceful park, now returning to its normal state.

With a final quack and a flap of wings, the last of the ducks waddled away, leaving Sean to enjoy the rest of his day in the quiet, beautiful park. But as he resumed his walk, he couldn't help but feel a little bit of joy at the unexpected and hilarious adventure he had just experienced. It was just another day in the life of Sean, where even a simple walk in the park could turn into a memorable and laugh-filled journey.

The tale of Sean's day, accompanied by a parade of peculiar ducks, became another delightful chapter in the town's endless collection of marvelous mysteries. The incident left the town buzzing with stories, as each witness carried a piece of that hilarious spectacle.

Chapter 11

The Bewildering Baguette Ballet

On this particular day, Sean was feeling all kinds of lucky and excited with his shiny new gold coin snuggled in his pocket. He thought, "What's a better way to celebrate my good fortune than with something sweet and scrumptious?" And off he went, like a kid on a mission, straight to the neighborhood's yummiest treasure chest - the bakery!.

The bakery, known in Limeridge for its delicious treats, was a cozy and inviting place. Its windows were always steamed up, giving it a warm, welcoming look. Inside, the smell of freshly baked bread and sweet pastries filled the air, making everyone's mouth water as soon as they walked in.

The bakery was lined with wooden shelves that proudly displayed a variety of bread - crusty baguettes, soft rolls, braided loaves, and more. The pastries were showcased in a glass counter, where croissants, donuts, and colorful cakes sat temptingly. The walls were decorated with pictures of bread and pastries, and a small chalkboard listed the day's special treats.

The baker, a jolly man with a flour-dusted apron and a constant smile, greeted everyone who came in with a hearty "Welcome!" He loved to chat with his customers, sharing stories and jokes, making everyone feel like they were part of the bakery family.

But on this particular day, as soon as Sean stepped into the bakery, things took a turn for the whimsical. It was as if his presence triggered a spell of magical mischief.

Suddenly, the loaves of bread and baguettes, which had been sitting quietly on their shelves, sprang to life. It was as if they had been waiting for just the right moment to show off their acrobatic skills. They flew off the shelves, twirling and swirling through the air. The baguettes spun like batons in a parade, and the loaves did somersaults and flips, making Sean's jaw drop in amazement and disbelief.

The pastries joined in too. Croissants rolled across the counter like little wheels, donuts hopped like frosted frogs, and the cakes did a wobbly dance, shaking their layers and decorations.

The baker, wide-eyed and as surprised as Sean, could only watch as his bakery turned into a playful circus of flying bread and dancing pastries. "Well, I've never seen them do that before!" he exclaimed, his surprise turning into laughter.

As the bakery transformed into this whimsical wonderland of flying bread, Sean found himself in a bit of a pickle. He tried his best to duck, dodge, and weave through the air full of bread, but it was like the loaves had a mission to play tag with him!

He moved left, and a crusty baguette zoomed right past his ear. He stepped to the right, and a soft, fluffy loaf gently smacked him on the back of the head. It was like a soft, doughy punch, and Sean couldn't help but burst into laughter.

The people in the bakery were having a ball watching the scene unfold. They stood with their coffees and pastries, chuckling and pointing as Sean danced around, trying to avoid the playful bread. "It's like a bread ballet, and Sean's the star!" one customer laughed.

A group of kids in the corner were giggling non-stop, their eyes following every move of the flying bread. "Look, that one's going for him again!" one child exclaimed, pointing at a sneaky sourdough that seemed to have taken a particular liking to Sean.

The scene was so absurd and hilarious that even Chaos, who had been cautiously observing from a safe distance, decided to join in. The cat leaped into the air, trying to catch a particularly frisky French loaf that was somersaulting above.

Sean, now fully embracing the chaos, started to play along. He pretended to be a goalkeeper, trying to block the bread with his hands, making exaggerated and funny faces each time he missed. The loaves, however, were gentle and soft, so each time one hit him, it was more like a playful nudge than anything else.

Then, WHAM! A big loaf hit Sean right in the face. He stumbled backwards and fell down, landing softly on the flour-dusted floor. The bread didn't stop; it kept coming, piling on top of him as if they were playing a game of hide and seek, and Sean was "it."

The baker stood there, his face as white as flour, amazed and confused. He couldn't believe what he was seeing—his bakery had turned into a circus, and the flying bread was the star of the show!

Trying to stand up, Sean wobbled and wiggled, but the rebellious bread was a squishy quicksand, not letting him escape its doughy grasp. Every attempt to rise turned into a funny flop, making the bakery a stage and Sean, the star of a slapstick comedy.

Desperate for freedom, Sean tried everything. He tossed pieces of bread, left and right, like a human catapult. He even nibbled at his soft attackers, hoping they'd retreat at the taste of defeat. But oh no, the bread was boldly bouncing, flipping, and flopping, keeping Sean in a funny fluster.

After a ballet of bumbles and tumbles, amidst a rain of crumbs, Sean decided it was time to wave the white flag. The bakery echoed with the giggles of this fluffy fiasco, as he stumbled out, leaving behind a battlefield of bread.

Although he had dreamt of a feast, Sean left the bakery, not as a triumphant pastry prince but as the giggling star of the great Bread Battle. The door closed, leaving behind tales of the mischievous muffins and the belligerent baguettes in the quirky kingdom of the bakery!

As Sean closed the bakery door, the bread started to calm down. One by one, the loaves and baguettes floated back to their shelves, settling down as if nothing had happened. The pastries rolled back into their places behind the glass counter, looking as innocent and delicious as ever.

Everyone in the bakery was swept up in the fun, laughing and joining in the playful chaos. The delightful spectacle turned the bakery into a lively and joyful place, filled with laughter and the spirit of playfulness.

As Sean walked out of the bakery, still chuckling from his encounter with the playful bread, the baker quickly hurried outside. In his hand, he held a fresh baguette, one that had not been part of the airborne chaos. He called out to Sean, who turned around, surprised.

"Here, Sean, take this one with you!" the baker said, holding out the baguette. It was golden-brown, crisp, and looked delicious.

"Oh, thank you!" Sean replied. He reached into his pocket, intending to pay for the baguette with one of his magical gold coins. As he pulled out the coin, something funny happened. The baguette in the baker's hand started to wiggle as if it recognized the coin's magic.

The baker's eyes widened in surprise. "Well, would you look at that!" he exclaimed. The baguette squirmed and wiggled like a happy puppy.

Sean, used to the quirks of his magical gold, tried to hand the coin to the baker, but the baguette's wiggling got even more energetic. It was as if the bread was saying, "No, not the magic coin!"

Seeing this, the baker laughed and gently pushed Sean's hand back. "No, no, you keep your coin, Sean. Just take the baguette. It's on the house!"

Sean smiled and put the coin back into his pocket, carefully taking the still slightly wiggling baguette. "Thanks, I will enjoy it!" he said.

The baker waved goodbye, still chuckling as he went back into his bakery. "You never know what will happen next with you around, Sean. You make Limeridge a brighter place!"

Sean waved back, now holding a baguette that had calmed down and seemed content to be in his hands. "Thank you! And thanks for the show today!" he called out.

As Sean walked away from the bakery, baguette in hand, he couldn't help but feel a sense of warmth and happiness. The magic of his gold coins had brought another unexpected and delightful moment into his day.

Walking down the street, Sean thought about the baker's kindness and the joy that seemed to follow him around in Limeridge. It was a town where even a simple trip to the bakery could turn into an adventure, and Sean was grateful for every magical moment of it.

He headed home, looking forward to sharing the baguette and the story of his day with his neighbors. In Limeridge, stories were always worth sharing, especially when they were as whimsical and heartwarming as this one.

Chapter 12

A Troublesome Decision

One quiet evening, Sean was lounging at home, sitting in his favorite armchair with Chaos, his loyal cat, curled up at his feet. The room was cozy, with soft light spilling from a lamp and casting a warm glow on the walls. Sean's gaze was fixed on the small pot of magical gold coins sitting on the shelf across from him.

"You know, Chaos," Sean started, breaking the silence, "these past few weeks have been something else. All because of these gold coins."

Chaos lifted his head, letting out a soft meow, as if he understood Sean's contemplation.

"The leprechaun wasn't joking when he said they were magical. But I'm starting to think 'troublesome' might be a better word," Sean continued, a half-smile on his face as he recalled the recent events.

He thought about the marching band that had shown up at his doorstep, the bakery turning into a circus of flying bread, and the ducks in the park acting like his personal cheerleaders. Each incident had been more bizarre and unexpected than the last.

"It's been fun, sure. But maybe it's a bit much. What do you think, Chaos? Should we go back to the forest and return these coins to the leprechaun?"

Chaos, who had seen his fair share of the coins' antics, gave Sean a look that seemed to say, "Maybe that's not a bad idea."

Sean nodded, as if confirming his own thoughts. "Yeah, maybe it's for the best. These coins... they're not just regular gold, are they? They're a bit of a handful."

He stood up and walked over to the window, peering out into the quiet Limeridge street bathed in the soft light of the streetlamps. The neighborhood was peaceful, a stark contrast to the chaos the coins had brought into his life.

"Life was simpler before, wasn't it, Chaos?" Sean mused, turning back to look at his feline friend. "We didn't have marching bands waking up the whole street or bread doing acrobatics."

Chaos meowed softly, as if agreeing with Sean's sentiment.

Sean walked back to his chair and sat down, picking up one of the gold coins and rolling it between his fingers. "I think it's time we said goodbye to these little troublemakers. Tomorrow, we'll go back to the forest and return them to the leprechaun. Maybe then things will go back to normal."

He placed the coin back into the pot and set it carefully on the shelf. "We've had our fun, but enough is enough. It's time to put an end to this magical madness."

Chaos purred, settling back into a comfortable position at Sean's feet.

Sean leaned back in his chair, feeling a sense of resolve. He was ready to part with the magical gold and the whirlwind of adventures it had brought. "Tomorrow's a big day, Chaos. We're going to set things right."

As he sat there, lost in thought, Sean couldn't help but smile at the memories. The gold coins had brought laughter, surprise, and a bit of magic into his life. But he knew it was time to let go and embrace the simpler joys of life in Limeridge.

He glanced at Chaos, who was now drifting to sleep, and whispered, "Goodnight, old friend. Tomorrow, we close this chapter."

With that, Sean turned off the lamp, leaving the room in soft darkness, the pot of gold coins shimmering faintly in the moonlight. It was the end of one adventure, but Sean knew that in a place like Limeridge, there was always another one just around the corner.

Chapter 13

Loop-De-Loop in Leprechaun Land

Sean, gripping the pot of gold firmly under his arm, ventured into Murphy's Forest, his mission clear but the path ahead filled with whimsy and unpredictability. "Mr. Leprechaun, where are you?" he called out, his voice echoing through the trees, bouncing here and there like a playful echo.

The forest seemed to be in a playful mood, responding to Sean's calls with its own set of giggles and whispers. The trees rustled as if they were sharing a secret joke among themselves, their leaves fluttering with what seemed like laughter.

Sean, undeterred, continued on his path, which twisted and turned like a maze designed by a particularly mischievous mind. He took a left, then a right, and then another left, but the elusive leprechaun was nowhere to be seen. It was as if Mr. Leprechaun was playing a game of hide and seek with him, always one step ahead, always just out of sight.

Chaos, who had followed Sean into the forest, seemed to be enjoying the adventure, his eyes wide with excitement as he darted ahead, then back, acting as Sean's scout.

As they walked, Sean couldn't help but admire the beauty of the forest. Sunlight streamed through the gaps in the trees, creating patches of light that danced on the forest floor. Birds chirped and sang, providing a cheerful soundtrack to their quest. The air was fresh and fragrant with the scent of pine and earth, making each breath feel like a gulp of pure nature.

"Come on out, Mr. Hide-and-Seek Champion!" Sean said, trying to peek behind bushes and up in the tall, teasing trees. He even asked a bird, "Hey, have you seen a leprechaun, about yay-high, green hat, filled with mischief?" The bird just winked, adding to the forest's playful mystery.

Chaos, who had insisted on accompanying Sean, trotted alongside him, his tail high in the air, looking every bit as determined as Sean. He occasionally stopped to sniff at a flower or chase a butterfly, adding a touch of comedy to their quest.

As they ventured further, the forest seemed to embrace them. The light filtered through the leaves in a kaleidoscope of greens and yellows, casting a serene glow over their path. The flowers seemed brighter, and the air felt fresher, as if the forest was aware of the importance of their mission.

The gold in the pot jiggled and jangled, almost as if it was giggling at Sean's topsy-turvy treasure hunt. It seemed like the gold coins were playing their own game of hide-

and-seek, flipping, and flopping around, creating a circus of sparkles.

Sean stopped by a babbling brook, the water twinkling as it flowed over the smooth stones. "Maybe the leprechaun is nearby," he thought, looking around. He placed the pot of gold down gently and called out again, "Mr. Leprechaun, it's Sean! I've come to return your coins!"

The only response was the gentle whisper of the forest and the soft gurgle of the brook. Sean sighed, feeling a bit silly but not giving up. He picked up the pot and continued his search.

At one point, Sean thought he saw a flash of green—a hat perhaps? He lunged toward the color, but instead of the leprechaun, he found himself face-to-face with a mischievous squirrel, munching on a nut. The squirrel, with cheeks full of food, gave Sean a look that seemed to say, "Looking for someone?" Sean groaned, thinking of the cheeky leprechaun. "Surely, this can't be part of his plan too?"

Taking a deep breath, Sean recalled the landmarks of their previous meeting. There was the moss-covered rock, the giggling stream, and that peculiar bush shaped like a dancing teapot! Ah-ha! He trotted off towards the dancing teapot bush, sure that he was on the right track.

As he reached the landmark, he found himself at the edge of a clearing. In the center was a large, twisted tree trunk. Sean approached cautiously, half-expecting the tree to burst into a fit of laughter. He knocked three times, remembering the old forest tales about secret tree doors.

To his surprise, a small window opened revealing... a disgruntled owl. "Whooo are you looking for?" it hooted, its feathers ruffled in annoyance. "Um, Mr. Leprechaun?" Sean replied hopefully. The owl rolled its eyes, "Typical! Everyone comes here looking for him. He's not here! Probably out creating more chaos."

Feeling slightly disheartened but not defeated, Sean decided to camp out, hoping to catch the leprechaun when and if he returned. As the night drew closer, Sean made a small campfire. The forest creatures seemed to gravitate towards its warmth and light. A group of playful rabbits brought him berries, and a kind deer even shared its cozy spot under a large fern.

"Maybe if we wait here, he'll come to us," Sean suggested, more to himself than to Chaos.

The evening turned into a mini-forest festival, with creatures sharing stories, and the firelight flickering to the beat of forest songs. Sean couldn't help but laugh at the irony. Here he was, trying to return the pot of gold, and yet, the forest gifted him with memories more precious than any treasure.

Sean looked up at the sky, visible through the canopy of leaves, and smiled. "Even if we don't find the leprechaun, this has been quite an adventure, hasn't it, Chaos?"

Sean leaned back against a tree, feeling at peace amidst the beauty of the forest. He closed his eyes, taking in the sounds and smells of nature, waiting patiently for the leprechaun to appear, and ready to return the magical, troublesome gold coins. Chaos meowed softly, curling up next to the pot of gold, his eyes slowly closing for a nap.

By morning, Sean was enveloped in a warm blanket of leaves, courtesy of the trees themselves. But there was still no sign of the leprechaun. Rubbing his tired eyes, Sean sighed.

Sean stood by the twisted tree trunk, which looked like it had come straight out of a fairy tale. He held the pot of gold in his hand and took out a piece of paper to write a note. "This seems like a good spot, right, Chaos?" he said, looking down at his cat Chaos who was busy inspecting a butterfly.

He scribbled down a message: “Dear Mr. Leprechaun, thanks for the adventure, but I want to give the pot of gold back. P.S. Next time, maybe just a pot of chocolate coins?” He chuckled to himself as he imagined the leprechaun reading his note.

But as he was about to place the note with the pot under the tree, a thought struck him. He turned to Chaos, who was now watching him with curious eyes. "Chaos, what if someone else finds these coins before the leprechaun does? What if the magic doesn't stop for us?"

Sean started to pace back and forth, the pot of gold still in his hand. "Or worse, what if Mr. Leprechaun doesn't find it at all? We can't just leave it here. That's a bad idea. A really bad idea."

Chaos meowed, as if agreeing with Sean's sudden realization. The last thing Sean wanted was for the magic of the gold coins to fall into the wrong hands, causing more chaos.

Sean looked around the forest, half expecting to see someone peeking from behind the trees, ready to snatch the pot as soon as he left. He hugged the pot closer to his chest, shaking his head. "No, no, no, we can't risk it. We'll have to find another way to return these coins to the leprechaun."

Chaos meowed again, and Sean nodded, feeling more confident in his decision. "We'll just have to keep looking for Mr. Leprechaun. Maybe he's playing hard to get, but we're not giving up that easily, are we?"

With a new sense of determination, Sean put the note back in his pocket and continued his quest through the forest, the pot of gold still safely under his arm. Chaos trotted alongside him, his tail high in the air, like a furry little knight on a quest.

As they walked, Sean imagined various scenarios of how they might finally encounter the leprechaun. "Maybe he'll pop out from behind a bush, or we'll find him taking a nap in a tree hollow," Sean mused aloud, his imagination running wild with possibilities.

The forest seemed to be in on the adventure too, with the leaves rustling and the birds singing, as if cheering them on. Every now and then, a squirrel would dart across their path, and Sean would half-jokingly ask, "Hey, have you seen Mr. Leprechaun?"

The search for the leprechaun turned into a fun game, with Sean and Chaos exploring every nook and cranny of the forest. They checked under rocks, behind waterfalls, and even in the hollows of old trees.

But as the sun began to set, painting the sky in shades of orange and purple, Sean realized that their quest for the day was coming to an end. "Looks like we'll have to try again tomorrow, buddy," he said to Chaos, who let out a soft meow in response.

Sean felt a bit sad because he couldn't find the Mr. Leprechaun in the forest. With the pot of gold still with him, he decided it was time to go back home. He hoped that no more crazy things would happen on his way back. Even though he was a little disappointed, Sean also felt happy carrying fun and silly memories from the forest. The forest was a funny place, always full of surprises and strange adventures! So, with a hopeful heart, Sean stepped out of the magical world of the forest, hoping to come and find Mr. Leprechaun again.

Chapter 14

The Never-Ending Road

The next morning, Sean was up bright and early, a determined look on his face. Today was the day he was going to return the pot of gold to the leprechaun. With Chaos by his side, who seemed to sense the importance of their mission, Sean grabbed the pot of gold and set off towards Murphy's Forest.

The sun was shining, the birds were singing, and everything seemed perfect for their little adventure. "Today's the day, Chaos! No more magical mishaps," Sean declared with a confident stride.

As Sean and Chaos began their journey to Murphy's Forest, the road ahead, usually so familiar and welcoming, took on a life of its own. It stretched endlessly ahead, winding and looping like a ribbon tossed by an invisible hand.

"Either I've forgotten the way, or this road's playing tricks on us," Sean mused aloud, scratching his head in bewilderment.

Chaos meowed in agreement, his tail twitching as if he too found the road's antics amusing.

They continued walking, expecting to see the familiar entrance to the forest at any moment. But instead, the path led them through a valley that was a complete mystery. The hills rolled like gentle waves in the sea, and fields of wildflowers nodded their colorful heads as if greeting them on their bizarre journey.

"Hello, flowers!" Sean waved, embracing the oddity of their situation. "Have you seen Murphy's Forest around?"

The flowers, of course, didn't respond, but their petals fluttered in the breeze as if chuckling at Sean's question.

Chaos, ever the intrepid explorer, darted through the flowers, his black and white fur a stark contrast against the vibrant colors of the valley.

The road twisted again, taking them up a hill that seemed to appear out of nowhere. As they reached the top, Sean expected to see the forest but was greeted instead by a panoramic view of more hills, valleys, and a distant sparkling stream.

"Wow, look at that view, Chaos!" Sean exclaimed, momentarily forgetting their mission. "It's like we've found a hidden part of Limeridge!"

Chaos sat down beside Sean, his green eyes taking in the view, his expression as close to awe as a cat's could be.

They continued their journey, the road leading them in loops and zigzags, like a playful snake. At one point, Sean was sure they had walked in a complete circle. "I think that rock is laughing at us," he said, pointing at a particularly large boulder they had passed twice already.

The boulder, covered in moss and dappled sunlight, did seem to have a face-like appearance, and in that moment, it looked like it was indeed chuckling at their plight.

As they descended another hill, the road suddenly split into two. Sean stopped, hands on his hips, looking from one path to the other. "Eeny, meeny, miny, moe," he chanted playfully, finally pointing to the left path.

Chaos meowed, as if in agreement, and off they went down the chosen path, which, to Sean's amusement, looped back to the fork in the road.

"Are we in a maze?" Sean wondered aloud, half expecting a Minotaur to appear.

They decided to take a break, sitting on a patch of soft grass by the side of the road. Chaos plopped down, his little paws tired from the unexpected adventure.

Sean laughed, shaking his head. "This road is more confusing than a maze. But at least it's a scenic maze!"

Chaos meowed, and they both sat there, enjoying the beauty of the unknown valley, the magic of the journey far outweighing the frustration of not reaching their destination.

Sean couldn't help but laugh at the absurdity of the situation. "It's like the gold coins have a mind of their own and don't want to go back," he joked.

Chaos let out a meow that sounded suspiciously like a chuckle. The two of them, a man and his cat, wandering aimlessly with a pot of gold – it was like a scene from a whimsical storybook.

Hours passed, and the road took them through different landscapes – a meadow filled with daisies, a grove of apple trees, and even a stretch that looked like a desert, complete with a cactus or two.

"We've seen more of the countryside today than we have in years," Sean remarked, trying to keep his spirits up.

"Who knew returning a pot of gold would be such an adventure?"

Chaos, who had started the journey with enthusiasm, now looked as if he was wondering what they had gotten themselves into. He trotted alongside Sean, his little paws getting tired.

As the sun started to set, painting the sky in shades of pink and orange, Sean realized that they were not going to find Murphy's Forest today. The magical gold coins, it seemed, had other plans.

Exhausted and a little bewildered, Sean decided to call it a day. "Looks like the leprechaun will have to wait, Chaos. Let's head back home and try again some other time."

They turned around and started the long walk back home. The road, which had taken them on such a wild and unexpected journey, now seemed to lead them straight back to Limeridge without any detours.

By the time they reached home, the stars were twinkling in the night sky. Sean set the pot of gold down with a sigh. "Well, that was an adventure and a half," he said, collapsing into his armchair.

Chaos jumped onto his lap, purring softly, as if to say, "We did our best."

Sean looked at the pot of gold, a mix of amusement and exasperation in his eyes. "You're more trouble than you're worth," he told the pot, but there was a smile on his face.

He leaned back, closing his eyes and thinking about the day's journey. It had been tiring, yes, but also full of laughter and unexpected beauty. "We'll try again, Chaos," he murmured. "But for now, let's enjoy some well-deserved rest."

And with that, Sean and Chaos settled in for the night, their hearts full of the day's adventures and their minds already wondering what tomorrow might bring in their magical, unpredictable town of Limeridge.

Chapter 15

The Flying Flowerpot Fiasco

The townsfolk of Limeridge were quite a sight to behold, especially when it came to their reactions to Sean's latest adventures. Picture this: their eyes were wide and round, like popcorn kernels bursting into fluffy white clouds at the slightest hint of another Sean escapade. It was as if their eyes were on springs, popping out in astonishment every time Sean walked by with a new story or a magical mishap.

Their laughter and giggles were like a simmering pot of soup, bubbling up and spilling over in a chorus of chuckles and chortles. Whenever Sean was around, it was as if someone had turned the heat up under this pot, making their giggles froth and bubble with excitement.

They would gather around, perching on whatever was nearby - benches, fences, or even the edge of the sidewalk, craning their necks and leaning in eagerly, not wanting to miss a single moment of the Sean show. Their expressions were a mix of disbelief, amusement, and sheer curiosity, all mashed together like a funny stew of emotions.

The children in the town were the most animated, jumping up and down with glee, their laughter ringing through the streets like bells. They would mimic Sean's adventures in their games, pretending to find magical pots of gold or talking to imaginary leprechauns.

The adults weren't far behind, often caught between trying to maintain a semblance of seriousness and succumbing to the infectious laughter that Sean's stories brought. They would exchange glances that said, "What will he do next?" while trying hard to suppress their own grins.

Even the local pets seemed to get in on the excitement. Dogs would bark happily, wagging their tails as if they too were waiting for the next chapter in Sean's book of wonders. Cats would watch from their perches, their tails twitching in anticipation.

All in all, the townsfolk of Limeridge were like characters in a colorful, lively cartoon, each waiting eagerly for the next episode in the ongoing series of 'Sean's Magical Adventures'. It was a circus of spectacular surprises, and Sean was the unwitting ringmaster, bringing joy, laughter, and a touch of magic to their everyday lives.

On one particularly nutty day in Limeridge, the sky decided to put on a show that was as unexpected as it was hilarious. It turned into a mischievous magician, and for its grand act? A swirling, twirling flowerpot extravaganza, with Sean as the unintended star.

There was Sean, just strolling along, minding his own business, probably thinking about what to have for lunch, when suddenly - BOOM! Out of nowhere, flowerpots began to tumble from the sky. But these weren't just any old flowerpots - they were dancing, diving, and doing acrobatics in the air. It was like they were playing a goofy game of "Catch if You Can" with poor Sean.

And they weren't just falling randomly. No, these flowerpots had a target, and that target was Sean. They zoomed and vroomed through the air, swirling around him as if they were part of a wacky, whirlwind parade.

Sean, caught by surprise, began a dance of his own. He twirled, he tangoed, and he jiggled like he was the lead in a slapstick ballet. “Whoa!” he cried out, ducking and weaving through the flowerpot frenzy. “This is nuts!”

Scratching his head, Sean couldn’t help but throw a giggle into the crazy salad of the day. "Did the sky forget to water its plants today, and now they're jumping ship?" he chuckled. It was like Mother Nature had turned into a comedian, and the flowerpots were her funny little helpers, turning the day into a carnival of craziness.

The townsfolk, witnessing this bizarre spectacle, couldn’t help but burst into laughter. There was Sean, doing a high-speed jig as he tried to dodge the playful pots. He leaped and bounded like a kangaroo on a caffeine buzz, his arms flailing, his legs jumping, all in an attempt to avoid the raining pots.

"Look at Sean go!" chuckled Mr. Thompson, the town's baker, as he watched from his shop window, a tray of bread forgotten in his hands.

Children giggled and pointed, their eyes wide with delight. "He's like a superhero dodging meteors!" one of them exclaimed, jumping up and down in excitement.

Even the local dogs joined in the fun, barking, and chasing after the flowerpots that landed on the ground, their tails wagging in amusement.

Chaos, who was usually so composed, looked on in astonishment, his tail puffed up, his eyes following each and every pot as it whizzed by.

As for the flowerpots, they seemed to be having the time of their lives. They twirled around Sean, some flipping over in mid-air, others doing loop-de-loops, as if they were auditioning for a circus act.

Finally, just as suddenly as it had started, the flowerpot fiesta came to an end. The last pot gently floated down, landing softly beside Sean, who was now panting and laughing, his hair tousled and his clothes covered in a smattering of soil and petals.

The townsfolk applauded and whistled, cheering for Sean's impromptu performance. "Bravo, Sean! Encore!" they shouted, their laughter echoing through the streets of Limeridge.

Sean, catching his breath, bowed dramatically, a big grin on his face. "Thank you, thank you! I'll be here all week," he joked, his eyes twinkling with mirth.

As he walked away, still chuckling to himself, Sean thought, "Just another ordinary day in Limeridge." And with that, he continued on his way, ready for whatever other wacky wonders the day might bring.

Chapter 16

The Elephant Extravaganza of Limeridge

In Limeridge, where ordinary days were as rare as a blue moon, a truly extraordinary event unfolded that would be talked about for years to come. This particular morning, the town didn't just wake up to the usual chirping of birds or the gentle breeze; it woke up to a thumping, bumping elephant parade!

Yes, you read that right. Elephants. In Limeridge!

These weren't just any elephants. They were big, goofy, and delightfully playful. They stomped and romped down the streets, their heavy feet making a rhythmic beat that sounded like a live drumming session. And who was leading this jumbo-sized jamboree? None other than Sean, the town's favorite son, who seemed to attract whimsical happenings like a magnet.

With a wide grin on his face, Sean guided the big-eared buddies through the streets of Limeridge. Each turn and each sidewalk became a new path of elephant fun. The elephants, with their massive bodies and swinging trunks, followed Sean like they were in the world's happiest conga line.

Their big, floppy ears wiggled with each step, and their mighty trunks swung from side to side, making the most amusing sounds - a mix of toots, honks, and happy trumpets. They danced and pranced along, their enormous feet going flippity-flop on the pavement, creating a spectacle that turned the whole town into a wonderland of elephant-sized joy.

The townsfolk, initially startled by the sight of elephants casually strolling down their streets, soon gathered to watch this incredible parade. People popped their heads out of windows, stood on their porches, and lined the sidewalks, their eyes as wide as pancakes. Their surprise quickly turned into laughter and cheer.

Children squealed with delight, jumping up and down, pointing at the elephants. "Mom, look at the funny elephants! They're dancing!" one little girl exclaimed, her laughter ringing through the air.

The local baker, Mr. Thompson, came out of his shop with a tray of fresh donuts, his mouth agape. "Well, I'll be! Elephants!" he gasped, but then he too joined in the laughter, offering donuts to the onlookers.

The elephants, seemingly aware of their audience, put on a show. One of them started to juggle apples with its trunk, while another played hopscotch on the street. A particularly cheeky elephant even picked up a garden hose and started spraying water, turning a patch of street into a mini water park for the delighted children.

"Look up there! It's not a bird, it's not a plane, it's Sean and his spectacular herd of elephant pals!" someone shouted, and the crowd erupted in cheers and applause.

Sean, acting as the ringmaster of this impromptu circus, couldn't help but laugh at the absurdity of it all. He waved to the townsfolk, feeling like he was in the middle of a dream. Chaos, who had been following at a safe distance, meowed and purred, his tail swishing in excitement.

As the parade continued, more and more people joined in the fun. The local marching band, upon seeing the elephants, couldn't resist joining in. They struck up a tune, and soon, the sound of trumpets, drums, and trombones filled the air, adding to the festive atmosphere.

The parade turned into a town-wide celebration, with people dancing on the streets, children riding on the elephants' backs, and laughter echoing off the buildings. It was a day of pure, unbridled joy, the kind of day that makes life worth living.

Eventually, as the sun began to set, painting the sky in hues of orange and pink, the elephants, as if on cue, began to march out of town, back to wherever they had come from. Sean waved goodbye to his big-eared friends, feeling a mix of happiness and disbelief.

The townsfolk lingered on the streets, not quite ready for the magic to end. They talked and laughed, recounting their favorite moments from the day.

As Sean walked home, with Chaos trotting beside him, he shook his head in amazement. "Only in Limeridge," he said to himself, a wide smile on his face.

That night, as the town settled down and the stars twinkled in the sky, Limeridge fell asleep with stories of elephants dancing in their heads, and Sean, the boy who led a parade like no other.

Chapter 17

The Great Milky Sail of Limeridge

On a morning that was about to become one of Limeridge's most talked-about tales, Sean woke up with a simple craving: milk. Little did he know that his magical gold coins had a surprise in store, turning his humble wish into an extraordinary, dairy-filled adventure.

As Sean rolled out of bed, ready to make himself a bowl of cereal, he noticed something peculiar. Instead of stepping onto his usual wooden floor, his feet met a cool, smooth surface that rippled and splashed under his weight. Blinking in disbelief, Sean realized he was standing in a river of milk!

His house had transformed into a milk-sailing ship, floating on a sea of milk that had taken over the streets of Limeridge. It was like a scene from a whimsical dream, with milk waves gently lapping against the walls of his house-boat.

"All aboard the S.S. Sean!" the townspeople shouted from their windows and doorsteps, laughing and clapping as they watched Sean's house-boat sail past. The spectacle was like a boat floating in a giant bathtub, except the bathtub was the town itself, and the water was pure, creamy milk.

Kids ran alongside the milky river, cheering and giggling. "It's like a giant milkshake!" one child exclaimed, eyes wide with wonder.

Adults chuckled and shook their heads in amusement. "Only in Limeridge," they said, watching the incredible scene unfold.

Sean, dressed in his pajamas, stood on the deck of his house-boat, a look of astonishment on his face. He had to admit, this was one of the most bizarre mornings he'd ever experienced. "I just wanted a glass of milk, not a whole river!" he called out, waving to his neighbors.

Chaos, ever the adventurous cat, prowled the deck of the Milk-Ship with curiosity, his paws leaving little creamy prints behind.

As the houseboat floated down the milky streets, it passed by familiar landmarks, all transformed by the sea of milk. The local park was now a milky lagoon, with ducks paddling around in the creamy liquid, looking quite pleased with their new environment.

The bakery, where Mr. Thompson stood in the doorway, his mouth agape, had become a milk-side café. "Would you like some donuts with your milk, Sean?" he joked, holding up a tray of freshly baked goodies.

The milk was smooth and flowed like a slow river, turning the town into a fairy-tale land. Flowers and bushes peeked out from the milk, creating a bizarre but beautiful landscape.

As the houseboat sailed past the town square, the marching band, never one to miss an opportunity for a performance, began to play a jaunty tune. They stood on a raised platform, their music adding to the festive atmosphere of the Great Milky Sail.

Children brought out their toy boats and floated them on the milky sea, pretending to be captains of their own milky ships. Dogs barked happily, lapping up the milk, while cats watched with cautious curiosity.

At one point, Sean's milk-ship sailed past a group of elderly ladies who were sitting on their porch, knitting. They looked up, their knitting needles pausing mid-stitch. "Well, I never thought I'd see the day when Sean sailed a milk river," one of them said, her eyes twinkling with amusement.

Sean, embracing the absurdity of the situation, decided to make the most of his milky voyage. He put on a captain's hat, which he found in his closet, and took the helm of his houseboat. "Full steam ahead!" he declared, steering the house down the creamy avenue.

The milk-ship's journey continued, with Sean waving to his neighbors and enjoying the surreal experience. The sun shone brightly, casting a soft, warm glow over the town, making the milk glisten like liquid gold.

Eventually, as all good things must come to an end, the milk began to recede, slowly draining away and leaving the streets of Limeridge as they were. Sean's houseboat gently came to rest back in its usual spot, as if it had never left.

The townsfolk gathered around, chatting, and laughing about the day's extraordinary event. Sean stepped off his now stationary houseboat, his feet finally touching solid ground.

"Well, that was one way to start the day!" he said, laughing along with his neighbors.

As the town returned to normal, the story of Sean's Great Milky Sail became a legend in Limeridge, a tale that would be told and retold with laughter and smiles. It was a reminder that in Limeridge, even the simplest wish for a glass of milk could turn into an adventure of fairy-tale proportions.

Every new day brought a fresh chapter in Sean's tale, filled with surprising and delightful occurrences. The people of Limeridge came to expect the unexpected, their lives brightened by the enchanting chaos of Sean's extraordinary journey.

Chapter 18

Lessons in Leprechaun Lingo

Every day, as reliable as the sunrise, Sean accompanied by Chaos could be seen trekking toward the enchanting edges of Murphy's Forest, the pot of gold secure under his arm. It had become a part of his daily routine, almost like a ritual. The pot, once a symbol of luck, now seemed like a cumbersome weight, a shiny burden that Sean carried with unwavering resolve.

The villagers of Limeridge couldn't help but take notice. They would peer over their garden fences and out from their shop windows as Sean passed by, the pot glinting in the sunlight. They leaned towards each other and whispered with a mix of sympathy and humor, "Off he goes again, to bargain with the forest!"

Children playing in the streets would pause their games to wave at Sean, some even calling out, "Good luck, Mr. Sean!" as he passed. Their parents would chuckle and shake their heads, thinking how the once ordinary Sean had become the town's most persistent adventurer.

Each time Sean returned, pot still in tow, the villagers would spy the hope fading from his face, replaced by a touch of exasperation. Yet, the next day, like clockwork, he would venture out once more, his spirit undiminished.

At the local café, over cups of tea and slices of cake, the villagers speculated about Sean's quests. "Do you think he'll ever find that leprechaun?" one would ask. "Maybe the leprechaun's moved to another forest!" another would suggest, causing a round of hearty laughter.

Even Mrs. Higgins, the town's oldest resident, found herself entertained by the spectacle. Sitting on her porch, knitting needles clicking away, she'd watch Sean with a twinkle in her eye. "The boy's got the persistence of a woodpecker," she'd remark to anyone who'd listen.

As days turned into weeks, Sean's attempts to return the gold became a beloved oddity, a part of the village's daily tapestry. His quest had turned into a communal tale of light-hearted folklore, a story that was embellished and recounted with each of Sean's departures and returns.

The villagers began to see Sean's quest as a reminder that some magic, however troublesome, brought a spark of excitement and wonder to their quiet lives. And so, they watched, they whispered, and they waited to see how the tale of Sean and his pot of gold would unfold.

Through it all, Sean never lost heart. He knew the villagers found humor in his plight, but he also felt their silent rooting for his success. Each trip into the woods, he carried not just the weight of gold but the collective anticipation of Limeridge.

Then, after countless days marked by the rhythmic pattern of Sean's determined footsteps heading towards Murphy's Forest, something unexpected happened. It was on a day that seemed just like any other, under the lush canopy of whispering leaves and dappled sunlight, that the leprechaun decided to make his long-awaited reappearance.

As Sean trod the familiar path, the weight of the gold feeling heavier with each passing step, he halted abruptly. There, materializing from a shimmer in the air, stood the leprechaun. With his emerald coat and hat askew, he appeared as if he had stepped out of a story, carrying with him the mischief and mystery of the old tales.

"Hello, Sean," the leprechaun greeted with a warm, teasing tone, a playful twinkle dancing in his eyes like the reflection of sunlight on a bubbling brook. "You seem quite eager to return the pot of gold. Tell me, why?"

Sean, caught off guard by the sudden encounter, blinked in surprise. The pot of gold, which he had been clutching tightly, now seemed to lose its weight as he gazed at the leprechaun. A mix of relief and curiosity filled his expression.

"Well, you see," Sean began, his voice a blend of earnestness and a hint of exhaustion, "Mr. Leprechaun, Its been quite an adventure, your gold is quite a handful! It's like carrying a pot of wacky wonders and troublesome tricks. But this pot of gold has brought more chaos than calm to my life, and to the town of Limeridge. I reckon we're not cut out for the kind of magic these coins seem to carry with them, Remember you mentioned it was no ordinary gold? You were right!"

Mr. Leprechaun nodded, his face a canvas of curiosity, "Oh, really? Do share the tales!"

And so, Sean spilled the stories of all that has happened in the last few weeks including the frogs, ducks, elephants, Milky way and Pickles so many pickles.

Mr. Leprechaun listened, his eyes dancing with the rhythm of each tale, but also flickering with a little flicker of sympathy. Sean pleaded, "Please, kind sir, take back your pot of golden mischief. My life has been a whirlwind of wonders, but it's time for calm skies."

"The joy and laughter they've brought were grand," Sean continued, a smile breaking through as he remembered the flying bread and the elephant parade, "but they've also turned my days upside down. I reckon a quiet life might be more my speed."

The leprechaun nodded, his eyes gleaming with a mix of amusement and understanding. "Ah, Sean, the magic of gold is indeed a tricky thing. It can bring wonders and jumbles, jigs, and tumbles. But it's not the gold itself that's important—it's the heart of the one who holds it."

Sean pondered the leprechaun's words, feeling the truth in them. He had been so focused on returning the gold that he hadn't considered the real magic was not in the chaos it created but in the stories and memories that would linger in the hearts of Limeridge's people.

"Perhaps," the leprechaun suggested with a sly grin, "you just need to find the right way to use it, or maybe, share it in a way that brings a different kind of magic to you and your neighbors."

Sean's eyes lit up, a new idea taking root. The leprechaun's words sparked a notion, a way to use the gold that could bring joy without the jumbles and tumbles.

"Thank you, Mr. Leprechaun," Sean said, a new resolve in his voice. "I think I know just what to do."

And with a nod of understanding, the leprechaun vanished as quickly as he had appeared, leaving Sean alone on the path with his pot of gold and a heart full of ideas.

As Sean walked back towards Limeridge, the villagers saw the familiar sight of him carrying the pot. Yet, there was something different this time—a look of inspiration, a spring in his step, and the beginning of a plan that would turn the troublesome treasure into a source of new magic for the whole town.

As Sean walked into town, clutching the heavy pot of gold, a sense of happiness and clarity washed over him. For so long, he had been plagued by confusion and turmoil, wondering why strange and unexplainable events had been occurring in their once-peaceful town. Now, he finally understood.

Initially, Sean had promised the town's people that he would share the wealth he found in the forest with everyone. However, he kept the gold for himself and kept of trying to spend it.

With the pot of gold in his hands, Sean called for a meeting with all the townspeople. Word spread quickly, and a crowd gathered in the center of town, their faces filled with a mix of curiosity and uncertainty.

"Ladies and gentlemen," Sean began, his voice carrying a hint of excitement, "you all remember the pot of gold, right? The one that brought us so much laughter and surprises."

The townspeople nodded, some with smiles and others with chuckles as they recalled the flying bread, the milk river, and the elephant parade.

"Well," Sean continued, "I've been thinking. I initially said I'd share the wealth with all of you, and I meant it. But somewhere along the way, I got caught up in the chaos and forgot about that promise."

The crowd listened attentively, a hush falling over them.

Sean held up the pot of gold, its shiny surface gleaming in the sunlight. "It's time to make things right. This gold doesn't belong to me alone; it belongs to all of us. Together, we can use it to make our town a better place."

Murmurs of agreement rippled through the crowd. They had always admired Sean's determination, and now they respected him even more for his honesty and generosity.

"So, here's the plan," Sean announced. "We'll use this gold to fund community projects, like repairing the old library, planting more trees in the park, and helping those in need. We'll turn these coins into a force for good, a source of happiness for everyone in Limeridge."

The townspeople cheered, their eyes shining with hope. They could see the potential for positive change, and it filled them with excitement.

As the days turned into weeks and the pot of gold was put to good use, the town of Limeridge transformed. The library, once dusty and forgotten, became a vibrant hub of learning and creativity. The park blossomed with new trees and colorful flowers, and families gathered there to enjoy picnics and play. Neighbors helped one another, and the sense of community deepened.

Through their shared efforts, the people of Limeridge discovered that the real magic of the gold was not in the chaos it could create but in the joy it could bring when shared with others.

And so, the town learned a valuable lesson about the power of generosity and cooperation. They realized that true wealth lay not in hoarding treasures but in using them to make the world a better place.

As for Sean, he continued to wear his mismatched clothes, his hair remained tousled, and his glasses still slipped down his nose. But now, whenever he looked in the mirror, he saw a man who had learned the importance of keeping a promise and the true meaning of wealth.

And the town of Limeridge? It thrived, not just with the shine of gold but with the warmth of hearts united in a common purpose—a purpose that had turned a pot of gold into a source of enduring happiness for all.

The End

About the Author

Sameer Mehra is a passionate writer with a diverse background and a love for storytelling. Inspired by a plethora of global encounters that have colored his life's canvas. Having resided in various corners of the world, he's soaked in a diverse melange of cultures, each leaving an indelible imprint on his soul.

As a voracious reader, he's always marveled at the magic of words to traverse realms. Transitioning from reader to raconteur, Sameer crafts tales, drawing deeply from his own rich trove of experiences.

Sameer's writing is a reflection of his multicultural journey. His work often explores themes of identity, belonging, and the human experience in a globalized world. Through his words, he aims to connect with readers on a profound level and inspire them to see the beauty in diversity.

The Unfortunate Luck of Sean O'Reilly

www.ingramcontent.com/pod-product-compliance
Lightning Source LLC
Chambersburg PA
CBHW050016170726
48282CB00025B/425
* 9 7 8 9 3 6 1 2 8 9 0 0 2 *